MONOMOTAPA
(RHODESIA)

MONOMOTAPA

(RHODESIA)

*Its Monuments, and its History
from the most Ancient Times to the present Century*

BY

THE HON. A. *Alexander* WILMOT

Member of the Legislative Council,
Cape of Good Hope

WITH PREFACE
BY H. RIDER HAGGARD

MAPS AND PLATES

NEGRO UNIVERSITIES PRESS
NEW YORK

Originally published in 1896
by T. Fisher Unwin, London

Reprinted 1969 by
Negro Universities Press
A DIVISION OF GREENWOOD PUBLISHING CORP.
NEW YORK

SBN 8371-1136-6

PRINTED IN UNITED STATES OF AMERICA

Dedicated to

THE RIGHT HONOURABLE CECIL J. RHODES

(MEMBER OF HER MAJESTY'S PRIVY COUNCIL,

ETC., ETC.)

WHO HAS BEEN PRINCIPALLY

THE MEANS OF

GIVING A NEW EMPIRE TO BRITAIN,

AND BY

WHOSE ADVICE AND AID

THE RESEARCHES INTO THE HISTORY OF MONOMOTAPA

WERE UNDERTAKEN.

INTRODUCTORY NOTE.

The great Zimbabwe ruins have been specially brought to public notice almost simultaneously with the conquest of the country in which they are situated, and a natural desire has arisen to read the riddle of this South African sphynx. It is desirable also to discover all possible traces of the history of the wonderful country of Monomotapa, the Ophir of King Solomon, and the land which is marked "rich in gold" in maps of the sixteenth and seventeenth centuries. I was commissioned by the Right Hon. Mr. Rhodes to make the best researches in my power in the archives and libraries of Europe. This has been done, and the treasures both of the Vatican and of Lisbon are used in the volume now laid before the public. Our best thanks are due to the Society of Jesus, some of whose learned men have rendered valuable assistance. All the treasures of the Vatican and the Archives of the Propaganda were freely placed at our disposal. We must publicly express our acknowledgments to Sir Luciano Cordeira, of Lisbon, for Portuguese and French works of great value and interest. The British South Africa Company, the Right Hon. Mr. Rhodes, and myself divide among us the cost of these literary researches.

Of course a work such as this has been undertaken and carried on amidst very serious difficulties. The pioneer in a foreign country is not to be judged by the same standard as the traveller on a well-beaten track. An honest attempt is made to give the best information obtainable, but many may be disappointed because impossibilities have not been performed. *Omne ignotum pro magnifico* applies to Monomotapa. When closely looked at, its Emperors become transformed into Kafir Chiefs, and its Palaces with gold-lined walls into clay huts.

An attempt has been made to produce a pioneer work of some interest and value, but it is a pioneer book, and therefore has some claim to indulgence. The narrative is only brought down to the year 1830, and therefore is not concerned with the conquests of the British South Africa Company.

A. WILMOT.

LONDON, *April*, 1896.

CONTENTS.

	PAGE
PREFACE	xiii

BOOK I.
PHŒNICIA 1

BOOK II.
ARABIA 77

BOOK III.
PORTUGAL 121

APPENDICES 223

PREFACE.

Southern and South Central Africa has been named the country without a past. Till within recent years its untravelled expanses were supposed from the beginning to have harboured nothing but wild beasts and black men almost as wild, who for ages without number had pursued their path of destruction as they rolled southward from the human reservoir of the north, each wave of them submerging that which preceded it. Within the last thirty or forty years, however, rumours arose that this was not true, or at least was not all the truth. Baines, and other travellers now dead, reported the existence of great ruins in the territories known as Matabele and Mashona Lands, and on the banks of tributaries of the Zambesi River, which from their construction must have been built by a race of civilised men; and in 1871 Herr Mauch re-discovered the fortress-temple of Zimbabwe, that now, as in the time of the early Portuguese, was said to be nothing less than the site of one of the ancient Ophirs.

It has been left, however, to the Hon. Mr. Wilmot, the author of this book, as a result of his patient searchings of the Vatican and other archives, to show that Zimbabwe was well enough known to the Portuguese between the years 1550 and 1700; that it was the home of the court of the so-called Emperor of Monomotapa; that a Christian Church flourished, or at any rate existed there; and that under the shadow of its ancient walls the protomartyr of South-eastern Africa, Father Gonçalvo Silveira, of the Society of Jesus, laid down his life in the service of the Faith. Afterwards it would seem that a new incursion of barbarians took place—how many such have those ruins witnessed? Probably these savages were of the Zulu section of the Bantu race; at least they stamped out whatever civilisation, Christian or Mahommedan, still flickered in Monomotapa so completely that even native tradition is silent concerning it, and once more oblivion covered the land and its story.

In 1891, after the occupation of Mashonaland by the Chartered Company of British South Africa, Mr. Bent, the learned explorer, visited the ruins of Zimbabwe and proved to the satisfaction of most archæologists that they are undoubtedly of Phœnician origin. There are the massive and familiar Phœnician walls, there the sacred birds, figured, however, not as the dove of Cypris but as the vulture of her Sidonian representative, Astarte, and there, in plenty, the primitive and unpleasing objects of Nature-worship, which in this shape or that are present wherever the Phœnician reared his shrines. There also stands the great building, half temple, half fortress, containing the sacred cone in its inner court, as at Paphos, Byblos, and Emesus. It is now ascertained moreover that within the walls of this temple men did not only celebrate their cruel and licentious rites, they also carried on their trade of gold-smelting. Here have been found crucibles and moulds for the refined metal and stones upon which it was burnished; indeed, the traveller has but to sift the soil to discover amongst it beads and other objects of pure gold. In a neighbouring ruin some two years ago a friend of the present writer, Mr. Burnham, unearthed, amidst the crumbling bones of men and the barbed arrow-heads of ancient make which in a past age had slain them, no less than six hundred ounces weight of gold, some of it in little flattened nuggets, as it had been beaten from the quartz, some melted together with the brazen vessels which contained it, in the conflagration that destroyed the building, and some in the shape of beads. More recently, as Mr. Wilmot mentions, another discovery of worked gold has been made, all of it showing traces of the skill of cunning and civilised jewellers, and in several instances ornamented with a deep incised pattern that is new to me. One of the gold beads found by Mr. Burnham I hold in my hand as I write. Unhappily it cannot tell its story, for if this were possible a most mysterious and fascinating chapter of history would be opened to us, as indeed may still happen should the explorers of the future have the good fortune to discover an undisturbed burying-place of the ancient inhabitants of Monomotapa. But, although such testimony is lacking, the many external evidences to which allusion has been made force the student to conclude, with Mr. Bent and Mr. Wilmot, that these buildings must have been constructed and that the neighbouring gold mines were worked by Phœnicians, or by some race intimately connected with them, and impregnated with their ideas of religion and architecture.

It is true, as Messrs. Chipiez and Perrot point out in their history of the art of this people, that no inland Phœnician town is known to history.* This does not, however, prove that none existed. Admitting that the inhabitants of Tyre, Sidon, and Carthage were exclusively seafaring traders, there is nothing to show that upon occasion they may not have penetrated to the interior of the countries which their navies visited, and even have settled there. Gain and slaves were the objects of the voyages of this crafty, heartless, and adventurous race, who were the English of the ancient world without the English honour, and at the ports of Eastern Africa, with which they

* "History of Art in Phœnicia," vol. i. p. 385.

doubtless trafficked, they must have learned that in the interior gold and slaves were to be won in abundance. It would seem that this temptation of vast profit caused them to break through their rule and march inland. But the distances and dangers of the journey, considerable even in these days, must then have been tremendous. A mere trading expedition was impossible; for it will be remembered that the servants of Solomon could not accomplish their visit to Ophir and return thence with the merchandise which was prepared for them, in a less time than three years. Moreover, as is the case to-day, the development and working of the inland mines by the help of native labour must have necessitated the constant presence and supervision of large numbers of armed and civilised men. It was therefore necessary that these adventurers, sojourning in the midst of barbarous tribes, should build themselves fortresses for their own protection, as it was natural that in their exile they should follow the rites and customs of their fathers. Doubtless in time the race became much mixed, for the women of the community must to a large extent have been supplied from the native peoples; but, as has been said and as is amply demonstrated in the following pages, it seems clear that its origin and characteristics were essentially Phœnician.

At what date this Phœnician occupation began, for how many centuries or generations it endured, and when it closed no man can say for certain, and it is probable that no man ever will be able to say. The people came, they occupied and built, they passed away, perhaps in some violent and sudden fashion such as might well have been brought about by a successful insurrection of their slaves, or by the overwhelming incursion of Arabian or more savage races. As Mr. Lang writes—

> "Into the darkness whence they came,
>   They passed, their country knoweth none,
>   They and their gods without a name
>   Partake the same oblivion.
>   Their work they did, their work is done,
>   Whose gold, it may be, shone like fire,
>   About the brows of Solomon,
>   And in the House of God's Desire.
>
> . . . .
>
>   The pestilence, the desert spear,
>   Smote them: they passed, with none to tell

> The names of them who laboured here :
>   Stark walls and crumbling crucible,
> Strait gates and graves, and ruined well,
>   Abide, dumb monuments of old,
> We know but that men fought and fell,
>   Like us, like us for love of gold."

Of the history of the ancient Zimbabwe and its long-lost wealth and glories we can gather no more than these scanty gleanings. The Arabs appear to have been acquainted with the place, but their geographers and historians tell us little, and it is not until the year 1560, or thereabouts, that, chiefly through the labours of Mr. Wilmot, the silence is broken. At this date, long after the Portuguese occupation of East Africa, Father Silveira, assisted by two colleagues, having successfully converted some minor chiefs in the coast regions, proceeded alone to the court of the Emperor of Monomotapa at Zimbaoe, or Zimbabwe.

What was the condition of this so-called empire, and what the measure of the effective dignity of its emperor, are points rather difficult to determine. The reader will form his own opinion upon them from Mr. Wilmot's pages, but they appear to have been much overrated by mediæval writers and geographers.

This monarch of Monomotapa, who after his conversion took the name of Sebastian, was, it is supposed, a heathen, but Mahommedans were present at his court, since a certain prelate, or *Imaum*, named Aligamus, or Mingames, who came from Mozambique, ultimately brought about the murder of the holy father. At first Silveira's labours seem to have been very successful, inasmuch as he baptized the emperor, his mother, and many of his nobles. But the tide soon turned; the *Imaum* Mingames persuaded the unstable Sebastian that Silveira was a wizard, and prevailed upon him to put him to death by murder. In the Appendix will be found a touching, and in the main obviously a truthful, account of this good man's martyrdom; also some interesting legends connected with his decease and the miraculous preservation of his body by wild beasts. So Father Silveira went the road which, had choice been given him, doubtless he would have chosen to tread, and now, more than three centuries after his death, it is suggested that he should be "beatified" by his Church. Thus ends his noble story in the world.

That the martyrdom of Silveira did not bring about the extinction of the Christian faith in Monomotapa is evident from a letter discovered by Mr. Wilmot in the archives of the Propaganda at Rome, which was written in 1630—that is, two generations after the tragedy—by the Dominican Father Louis at Goa to the Provincial in Portugal. From this document it appears that the Emperor of Monomotapa of that day organised and executed a massacre of all the Christians in his country, among them the ambassador sent to his court by the "captain of Mozambique." Thereupon Father Louis, who was a Christian militant, "for the love of our Lord and honour of religion," put himself at the head of an army of fifteen thousand men, and advancing to a place named Mocapa, in either one or two battles attacked and routed the host of the emperor, which numbered a hundred thousand men, killing the greater part of the "grandees of the empire." Marching in triumph to Zimbabwe, Father Louis crowned Manura, an uncle of the defeated monarch, making him tributary to the "Catholic King." Further, he built and dedicated a church to the Blessed Virgin of the Rosary, and converted the new king and his wife to the Christian Faith.

Having accomplished these great deeds, the father seems to have returned to Goa, since he writes of them thence two years later. On receipt of his report ten missionaries were sent from Portugal to Monomotapa, but what became of them we cannot tell, for now again the gloom gathers around the old city of Zimbabwe. Doubtless behind its veil many sanguinary events took place, among them the destruction of the empire of Monomotapa by savage hordes and the forcing back of the Portuguese to their settlements on the coast.

Now, after the lapse of another two centuries and a half, that veil has been lifted once more by the bold enterprise of the British South Africa Company, and the crumbling temple of Zimbabwe, the scene of so much forgotten history and of so many unwritten tragedies, by a strange chance has received the bones of the heroic band of Englishmen who fell with Wilson on the banks of the Shangani river. It is legitimate to hope, it seems probable even, that in centuries to come a town will once more nestle beneath these grey and ancient ruins, trading in gold as did that of the Phœnicians, but peopled by men of the Anglo-Saxon race. With every modern student of history the future inhabitants of that town and of the surrounding territories, will be grateful to the Hon. Mr. Wilmot, through whose research such of its mediæval records as remain to our own day have been disinterred from the forgotten archives of the Vatican and Lisbon and given to the world in the pages of this book.

H. RIDER HAGGARD.

May 1, 1896.

BOOK I.

PHŒNICIA.

NOT only in South-eastern Africa have the oldest mines in the world become the newest gold fields, but it has devolved upon the newest development of British Imperialism to bring to light interesting monuments of one of those ancient peoples of the world whose history is almost lost in the distance of remote antiquity. Herr Mauch may be said to have rediscovered the colossal ruins of Zimbabwe in 1871, and since then they have been well and faithfully described by Mr. J. T. Bent.*

* "The Ruined Cities of Mashonaland, being a Record of Excavation and Exploration in 1891. By J. Theodore Bent, F.S.A., F.R.G.S.; with a chapter on the Orientation and Mensuration of the Temples by R. M. W. Swan, London. Longman and Co., 1892."

As Mr. Selous points out, the title "Ruined Cities" is a misnomer as applied to ruins of detached forts, &c. On

In "Seven Years in South Africa," by Dr. Emil Holub, he describes a ruin on the Shashi river composed "of blocks of granite, laid one upon another without being fixed by cement of any kind." Speaking at the Royal Geographical Society meeting on November 24, 1890, Mr. G. Philips, who had lived in the country for years, said that the Zimbabwe ruins were exactly like others he had seen in South-east Africa between the Limpopo and Zambesi rivers. Of the ruins at one place near Tati, he says: "The walls are twelve to fifteen feet thick, and it is entered by a passage so arranged as to be commanded by archers from the interior and it only admits of the passage of one at a time." Once, when hunting, he came on a regular line of these ruins with zigzag patterns and mortarless walls of small hewn stones. He says: "One must have been a tremendously big place. There were three distinct gateways in the outer wall, which I suppose was at least thirty feet thick at the base, and one of these immense iron wood trees that would have taken hundreds of years to grow, had grown up through a crevice in the wall and rent it asunder." So far as ruins at Tati and on the Impakwe are concerned, Mr. Maund, quoted by Mr. Bent, tells us: "As I have said, these ruins are always found near gold workings; they are built in the same way, of granite hewn into small blocks somewhat bigger than a brick, and put together without mortar. In the base of both of these there is the same

---

the subject of these ruins see Mr. Selous' paper read before the Royal Geographical Society, as also his last work on South Africa. The subject is also referred to in "The Story of the Expansion of South Africa," by the author of the present work.

herring-bone course as at Zimbabwe, though nearer the base of the wall. . . . The remains on the Impakwe are similar in construction, and are within fifty yards of the river; it was evidently an octagonal tower." Mr. Bent tells us that "There is another ruin of a similar character near where the river Elibi flows into the Limpopo, and another further up the Mazoe valley than the one we visited." Monteiro and Gamitto, who travelled to the Zambesi in 1831-2, refer to many "Zimbabwes," or ruins of ancient forts, which they heard of and saw. Ruins at Gwelo have just been discovered (1895).

Under the auspices of the Royal Geographical Society, the British Chartered Company, and the British Association for the Advancement of Science, Mr. Bent as an archæologist has performed excellent pioneer work. He has found sermons in the stones of colossal remains, or at least texts from which valuable inferences can be drawn, so as to guide us, by no uncertain light, to a knowledge of the truth. We will unreservedly follow his description because it is the best, but it is well to bear in mind that what is described is only a fraction of what exists, and that new ruins are constantly in course of discovery. "The Great Zimbabwe," however, is situated in the territory of the British South Africa Company between the Limpopo and Zambesi rivers, far inland, and 3,300 feet above sea level in latitude 20° 16′ 30″, and longitude 31° 10′ 10″ E. Built of granite rock on a granite foundation, the ruins of the fortress are composed of rough blocks of stone put together without mortar. Situated on the top of a hill and protected on the south by a precipice ninety feet high, the position is made still stronger by being protected in one direction by gigantic granite boulders, while on the only accessible side a wall of massive thickness was erected. We are told that "this wall is thirteen feet thick on the summit, with a batter of one foot in six; it is thirty feet high in parts, and the flat causeway on the top was decorated on the outside edge by a succession of small round towers alternating with tall monoliths; seven round towers in all we made out, about three feet in diameter, and several others had been destroyed by the fall of a portion of the wall. . . . The labyrinthine nature of the building baffles description. In one place is a narrow sloping gully, four feet across, ascending between two boulders, and protected for no conceivable reason by six alternate buttresses and a wall at the upper end, forming a zigzag passage narrowed in one place to ten inches. Walls of huge size shut off separate chambers. In all directions everything is tortuous; every inch of ground is protected by buttresses and traverses. . . . On a portion of the wall outside ran a dentelle pattern formed by placing the stones edgeway. . . . To the south of 'The Temple' a flight of steps led down to the gold-smelting furnaces and the caves. Here there is an enormous mass of fallen stones from the buildings above. . . . Vainly one tries to realise what this fortress must have been like in the days before ruin fell upon it, with its tortuous and well-guarded approaches, its walls bristling with monoliths and round towers, its temple decorated with tall weird-looking birds, its huge decorated bowls, and in the innermost recesses, its busy gold-producing furnace." Mr. Bent proves that these buildings were erected by people who practised the nature worship of Phœnicia. On many stones the phallus is either realistically or conventionally represented, while numerous towers and pillars are of the same character; the birds (vultures or hawks) represent Astarte, the female element in Creation, and there are rosettes (emblems of the Sun) used in the same way as on the Phœnician sepulchral stelæ in the British Museum. Not only are round towers and monoliths especially deserving of attention, but many peculiar round blocks of dolorite. Mr. Bent tells us: "The collection here of so many strange geological fragments cannot be accidental, and points to the veneration of curious-shaped stones amongst the earlier inhabitants of the ruins, which were collected here on the platform, a spot which I am convinced will compare with the Bartuhra or Betyles of the Phœnicians, and of this stone cult we have ample evidence from Arabia." *

* The reader's special attention is called to this paragraph, as in due course the subject of stone worship in connection with the history of these ruins will be referred to. Mr. Bent (p. 163) very truly says, "El Masoudi alludes to the stone worship of Arabia, and leads us to believe that at one time this gross fetichism formed a part of the natural religion of the Semitic races. Marinus of Tyre says they honoured as a god a great cut stone. Euthymeus Zygabenus further tells us that, apparently, "This stone was the head of Aphrodite, which the Ishmaelites formerly worshipped. . . . When the Saracens were converted to Christianity they were

The fragmentary lettering discovered on one stone compares curiously with the proto-Arabian type of lettering used in the earlier Sabæan inscriptions. The circles on the birds also appear to have a line across, like the fourth letter given as illustrating the early Arabian alphabet. Soapstone cylinders decorated with rings of knobs were discovered exactly similar to Phœnician objects of the same character found at Paphos in Cyprus. They remind one of Herodian's description of the sacred cone in the great Phœnician temple of the Sun at Emesa in Syria, which was adorned with certain knobs or protuberances, a pattern supposed by him to represent the Sun, and common in phallic decorations." Evidence of ancient cult, ancient construction,

obliged to anathematise the stone which they formerly worshipped (see 'Akadamie der Wissenschaft,' Wien, 1890). Herr Kremer in his account of the ancient cult of Arabia makes frequent allusion to the stone worship. In the town of Taif a great unformed stone block was worshipped identical with the goddess which Herodotus calls Urania; and one must imagine that the Kaaba stone at Mecca resembles the black schistose block which we found at Zimbabwe. It is an exceedingly old-world worship, dating back to the most primitive ages of mankind."

and ancient art, forces Mr. Bent to the conclusion that the gold fields of Mashonaland formed at least one of the sources from which Arabia obtained its gold.* In fact, South-

* The extraordinary manner in which the Phœnician races penetrated to the most remote regions of the world in search of wealth, whether by means of commerce or mining, is illustrated by the ingot moulds of soapstone found at Zimbabwe. Mr. Bent says (p. 182): "In the adjoining cave we dug up an ingot mould of soapstone of a curious shape, corresponding almost exactly to an ingot of tin found in Falmouth harbour which is now in the Truro museum, and a cast of which may be seen at the School of Mines in Jermyn Street. This ingot of tin was undoubtedly made by Phœnician workmen, for it bears a punch mark thereon like those usually employed by workmen of that period; and Sir Henry James in his pamphlet describing it draws attention to the statement of Diodorus that in Ancient Britain ingots of tin were made of the shape of *astragali*, or knuckle bones." (A joint-stock syndicate has succeeded in obtaining quantities of gold beads and gold wire from the Zimbabwe ruins, part of which have been seen by the author at the offices of the British South Africa Company, St. Swithin's Lane, London. The beads are round, of a uniform simple pattern, and vary in size from almost microscopic dimensions. The wire is in considerable lengths, and, it is presumed, was used for bracelets and other ornaments.) The manner of mining of the Phœnicians is shown in old workings in Leinster, in Ireland, and there now can be but little doubt that the "round towers" of that country are attributable to Phœnicians, or to those at least who were followers of the religion they introduced.

eastern Africa was an "Ophir;" and he adds that, in his opinion, "The cumulative evidence is greatly in favour of the golddiggers being of Arabian origin, before the Sabæo-Himyaritic period in all probability, who did work for, and were brought closely into contact with, both Egypt and Phœnicia, penetrating to many countries unknown to the rest of the world.*

Knowing that the Zimbabwe forts of South-eastern Africa were erected by a Phœnician

* Mr. Bent says by way of argument (p. 186): The Bible is full of allusions to the wealth of Arabia in gold and other things. Ezekiel tells us that the Sabæans were merchants in gold for the merchants of Tyre. Aristeas tells us that a large quantity of spices, precious stones, and gold were brought to Rome by the Arabians. Universal testimony proves that little or no gold could have come from the peninsula itself. Egyptian monuments also indicate the wealth of the people of Punt, and the consensus of opinion places this kingdom in Yemen, south of Arabia. "It would seem to be evident that a prehistoric race built the ruins in this country . . . like the mythical inhabitants of Great Britain and France who built Stonehenge and Carnac." After all, Stonehenge is a Phœnician temple, and, although records of Ancient Phœnicia and Arabia scarcely exist, it cannot be said that the Phœnicians are a prehistoric people. In the context we will endeavour briefly to trace the faint outline of their history, preserved to us by means of inscriptions and other records.

people, one question which naturally arises is, What was their original form? They must have been much more extensive than at present, because of the enormous heaps of stones which have evidently fallen from them. A tradition exists, which is mentioned by Portuguese chroniclers, that they were destroyed by an earthquake in the fifth century, and certainly the nature and character of the ruins renders this explanation somewhat probable. Large masses of masonry have been hurled as from a height, and it is difficult to conceive that any action of man could have effected this result. It does not seem either that the materials of the forts were ever required by nations who made huts their dwelling-places; besides it must be remembered that strongholds of defence were always places of prime consequence, and at no time would have been dismantled for the purpose of erecting temples or any other edifices.

One of the first and most natural questions is, What was the ancient form of these forts? An answer may possibly be discovered by means of considering the nature and character of Phœnician fortresses in other parts of the world. We know that this great maritime nation spread their sails over all portions of the Mediterranean Sea. Not only did they found Carthage in the north of Africa, but placed colonies in Cyprus, Sicily, Malta, and Sardinia. In the last-mentioned island there are remains of buildings strikingly like the Zimbabwes of South-eastern Africa, and their careful consideration may therefore be useful.

In the Nauraghe of Sardinia is a tower in the form of a truncated cone (see Fig. 1). It is constructed with blocks of stone. In some cases they seem to have received shaping from the hand of the builder, but in most instances it is not so. Invariably they are piled on each other without any mortar being used. The entrances are generally so low that it is necessary to go in on hands and feet. On entering we find round, and occasionally elliptic, chambers which are sometimes six to seven metres in height. The passages are designed in a parabolic form, and form a sort of elongated dome, of which the diameter measures four or five metres. One of the Nauraghes, styled Nieddu, furnishes a type

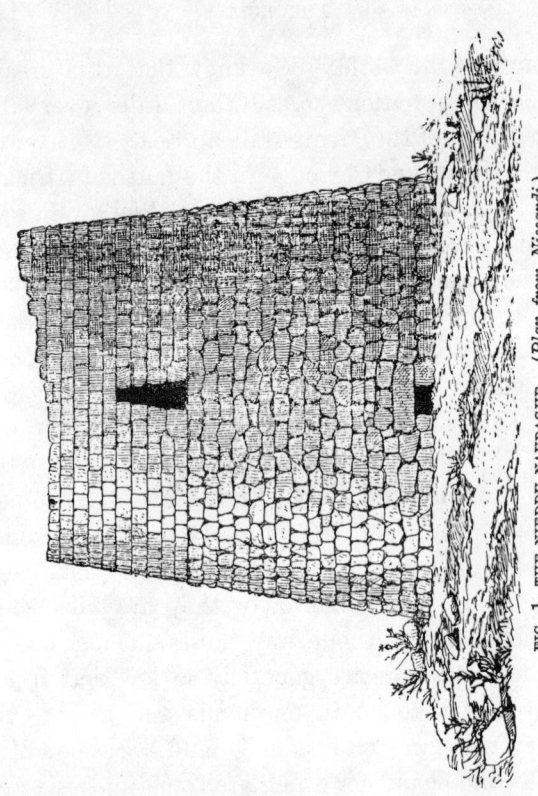

FIG. 1. THE NIEDDU NAURAGHE. *(Plan from Nissardi.)*

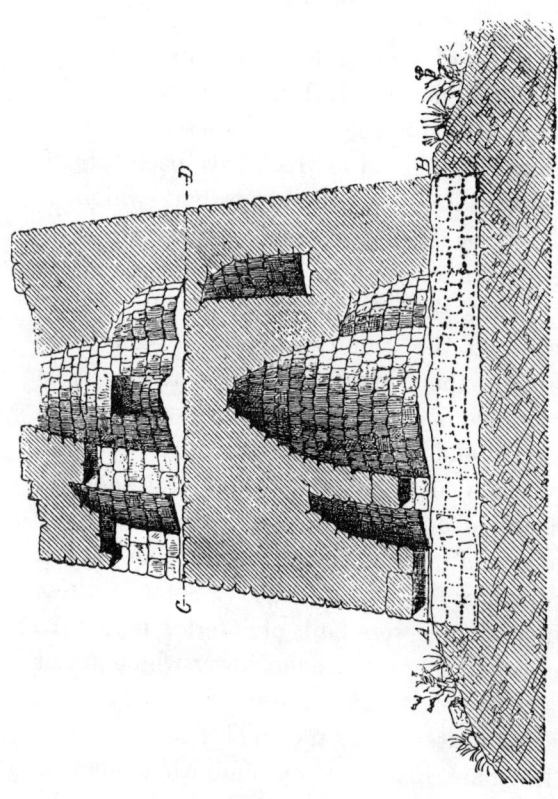

FIG. 2. THE NIEDDU NAURAGHE. LONGITUDINAL SECTION. (*From Nissardi.*)

of a tower of two stages. The upper portion was sometimes reached by a narrow spiral staircase within the wall. These towers, if we can judge by those which have been spared, all terminate in a circular terrace which is reached by the staircase. Almost all have their entrance towards the south-east. It is calculated that three thousand Nauraghes existed in the island of Sardinia, and there is among them great varieties, particularly so far as size is concerned, although with regard to type and general character one of them represents all. Isolated towers and those of a massive conical description are frequently found, and in some cases the latter is flanked by three or four lesser towers. Some of these minor edifices were built of inferior materials. Here and there the cone tower which forms the centre of the construction is much larger than the exterior towers which flank it.

In some instances we find what may be styled an agglomeration of Nauraghes in the form of a hill fortress as shown in the accompanying picture (Fig. 3) of the Nauraghe de Sarecci from the "Atlas" of La Marmora.

This is one of the largest of the ruined

FIG. 3. THE SARECCI NAURAGHE. PERSPECTIVE VIEW.

fortresses of Sardinia, and is about two hundred metres in circumference, nevertheless it is not so complicated as the Nauraghe Ortu. This building is styled the King of Nauraghes, and is well known to have possessed two higher stages.

A Sardinian architect named Cima, whose devoted and intelligent study of these ruins fitted him for the task, was able at last to publish an attempt to show this fort as originally built. This is shown in Fig. 4.

The lowest stage of this large edifice was composed of ten chambers, which did not include the little cells of the great central chamber. It had four courts, one of which was very small, and entrance was obtained by four gates from which people were able to proceed by eleven different interior openings. All the great Nauraghes possessed passages between the massive central wall and the wall flanked by towers. The Nauraghes are found generally on the slopes of mountains or on the summits of hills. It is rare to find isolated ruins in one of the cantons of the island. In such cases it has been frequently found that after a careful search other ruins,

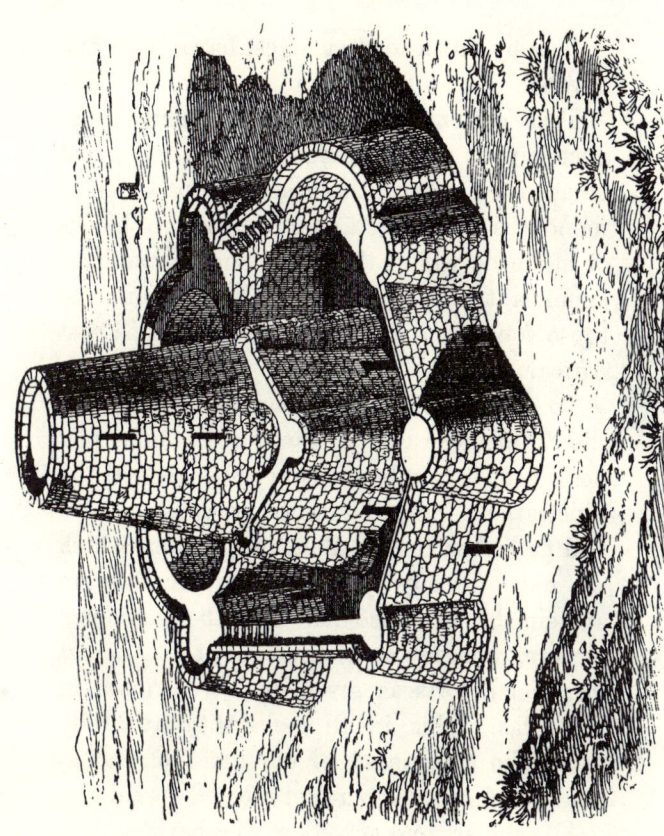

FIG. 4. THE ORTU NAURAGHE, RESTORED BY CHAS. CHIPIEZ.

hidden by brushwood or trees, have been discovered.

Two circumstances of consequence connected with the Nauraghes of Sardinia must be adverted to, and these are the presence of monoliths (see Fig. 5), and of rough blocks of stone on which there are phallic emblems significant of nature worship, and similar to those found at the Zimbabwes of South-east Africa.

To show by pictures the great similarity of the Zimbabwe ruins to those in Sardinia just described, it is only necessary to glance at the illustrations prepared with scrupulous care and published by Mr. Bent in the work which we have already quoted from. A few are subjoined. We also show in the subjoined pictures the reconstruction of the ancient Phœnician forts as given by La Marmora in his Atlas. This in all probability truthfully shows the appearance of our great Mashonaland monuments when first erected.

All scholars and travellers who have studied the subject of the Sardinian ruins have naturally encountered the problem concerning the object for which they were built. Four hypo-

FIG. 5. RAISED STONES. (*From La Marmora.*)

theses have been proposed, each of which has been examined with great care. The most ancient idea was that the Nauraghes were

FIG. 6. THE ZURI NAURAGHE, NEAR ABBASANTA.
(*From Baux.*)

tombs, but it has been replied, if this be so, Why have no remains of bodies ever been found after many years of very strict and diligent research? It has been asked, if the Nauraghe was a tomb, Why these superposed chambers; why the staircase ascending to the upper platform? * There is no tradition here of any veneration for the tombs of the dead. On the contrary, there are places

FIG. 7. EXTERIOR VIEW OF DOORWAY OF THE ZURI NAURAGHE.
(*From Baux.*)

in the neighbourhood known in Sardinia as

* "Histoire de l'Art dans l'Antiquité," par Georges Perrot et Charles Chipiez, Membres de l'Institut, &c., tome iv., Paris, 1887, pages 37 *et seq*. The description of the Nauraghes has been taken from this valuable work, in which there are ample quotations from La Marmora, "Voyage en Sardaigne," "The Atlas of Marmora;" "La Sardegna, par M. Pais," and many other writers.

FIG. 8. GENERAL VIEW OF ZIMBABWE.

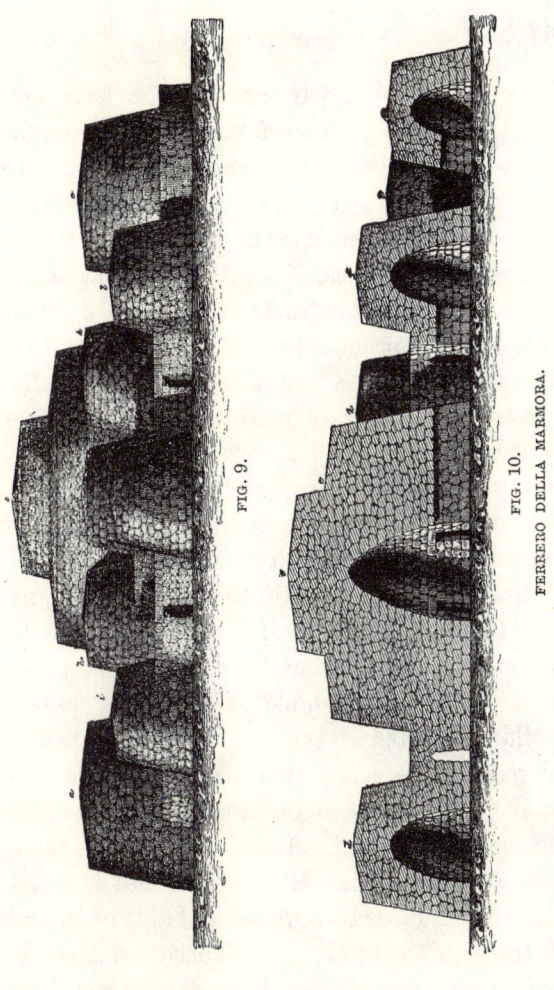

FIG. 9.

FIG. 10.

FERRERO DELLA MARMORA.

the "Tombs of the Giants." Why have not the places of sepulture of these ancient people been sought for in the Nauraghes? "It is not admissible that these two types so different should be formed for the purpose of satisfying one and the same want; . . . that these great buildings constructed of blocks of stone without mortar should serve two purposes. . . . It is desirable to renounce the search for graves in the Sardinian Nauraghe because we possess them in the 'Tombs of the Giants.'"

Can these ancient buildings have been temples? To this it is replied, that one first objection which presents itself to the mind is that there would really have been too many sanctuaries for the half-barbarous people to whom we must attribute the erection of these edifices. "The temple is always a public building erected at the public expense, which is required to serve all classes of people who wish to meet there on certain days for the accomplishment of certain rites. How, then, can we explain that fifty—sometimes as many as two hundred—temples should be found within one canton? . . . These edifices do not seem to us to be planned for assemblies and for religious ceremonies. The inconvenience of the entries and the obscurity in which the chambers are plunged, seem repugnant to this conjecture. . . . We believe that there was a sanctuary, but certainly that this was not in a fortress."

The plans point to there having been outside the Nauraghes great courts of a circular character and "open to heaven," in which worship took place. In fact, there were altars near the conical towers and "high places" where the Phœnician system of religion was practised as in Syria.

We are told that the "houses where the constructors of the Nauraghes lived were cabins," and that the Nauraghes were the fortresses where they kept their arms and precious objects. These were their places of asylum, where they took refuge in danger. From the height of the terrace which looked over the country they could see their enemy from afar, and by means of signal fires neighbours and friends could be warned. Fortified upon this platform they launched their weapons upon the aggressor. They caused heavy stones to roll upon him if he approached too near in order to force the narrow and low entry. It was besides easy to block passages, as some big stone reserved for this purpose would suffice to obstruct it. In narrow passages, which could even allow of wooden barricades, two or three men would have been able to defy an entire troop. In order to reduce the place the assailant had only to trust to famine, if he did not possess the immense machines capable of making an impression upon massive thick walls. In the large Nauraghes an entire tribe found an asylum, and even then flocks could be taken into the interior. If the isolated Nauraghe of small dimensions presents to the historian an enigma which appears at first almost insoluble, the question becomes cleared up when we take the same type arrived at its full development. Then doubt is no more permitted. We divine the idea and the sentiment which have given birth to the Nauraghe. In a social state which was insecurity itself— where there was almost, without ceasing, war between families, war between the tribes of the same race, and, above all, between the tribes of different races, each constituted group, whether family or tribe, wished to have a place of refuge where it was able to shut itself up and resist attack. The same phenomena is reproduced at all times in the midst of similar troubles. Recall the towers of the Middle Ages, those which are still erect among the houses of Bologna, or which more numerously exist in Tuscany. "In Greece I have seen villages, such as Vetylo, where each chief of a family, if he were thirty years of age, had his *pyrgos* carefully reserved. This was a high and massive tower, at the foot of which there were dwelling-places. Old men have told me that in their youth, before Otho came to the crown, they often left the low and accessible parts of their dwelling to barricade themselves in the *pyrgos*. . . . The Nauraghe was the *pyrgos* of Sardinia, of the chief of the family, or, when the building was of considerable dimensions, of the chief of the tribe; this was the centre of the village, and in the case of alarm, the resource and the asylum of those who inhabited it. Around it were grouped houses more lightly built and more open. . . . The workshops where they made their arms and other utensils of bronze were near. . . . Finally, there was in the shade of the Nauraghe, if we may use the term, the place where their ancestors slept: 'The Towers of the Giants' have been mostly found in the immediate vicinity of towers destined to protect the living. . . . The Nauraghe represents a very peculiar type of elementary and primitive architecture, a type which the most ancient inhabitants of Greece have seen without developing it; . . . the Balearics have their talayots (a diminutive of a word which means a tower of observation); . . . 'they have the same plan, the same form of truncated cone.'

"In what epoch were the Nauraghes of Sardinia built? We do not know. Near the ruins of Nora, at the south of the Gulf of Cagliari, the arches of a Roman aqueduct are supported upon the massive base of a Nauraghe. . . . The ancient *truddhus* of Italy are striking in their resemblance to Sardinian ruins. They consist of massive conical towers, examples of which are found in Otranto."

The age of these towers goes back to a remote antiquity—to the Bronze Age—to a time when the Romans were not known on the Tiber, and before the Carthaginians had erected an empire in the north of Africa.*

There are two distinct descriptions of ruins at the great Zimbabwe in South-eastern Africa described by Mr. Bent. We have already referred to the forts, and must now take the description of the "temple." Beneath the Hill fort is a circular building, whose ground plan is given.

* For quotations in the text see " Histoire de l'Art, par Perrot et Chipiez, tome iv., Paris, 1887." Pictures of the Nauraghes and objects of interest found in Sardinia are contained in " Des Gesammette Akademische," which the Academy of Berlin published in 1866. At p. 6, vol. ii. of the re-impression of this work, Gerhard says: " I have no hesitation in considering the numerous round edifices of Sardinia which are known under the name of Nauraghes as monuments of the worship of Baal, adored as the divinity of fire." He does not believe in the hypothesis that these monuments ought to be attributed to the primitive population of the island. Gerhard (quoted by Perrot et Chipiez) recognises the Sardinian idols referred to by La Marmora as Carthaginian gods very much resembling Baal, Moloch, and Astarte. Upon this Perrot and Chipiez ("Histoire de l'Art," tome iv. p. 9) tell us that at Cagliari the names of the artists are known who forged antiquities for General La Marmora. See also M. Pais, "La Sardegna prima del Dominio Romana, Rome, 1881." The view taken by the great French writers whom we have followed is that the Nauraghes are attri-

Mr. Bent tells us (p. 92) that "What appeared at first sight to be a true circle eventually proved elliptical—a form of temple found at Marib, the ancient Saba and capital of the Sabæan kingdom in Arabia, and at the Castle of Nakab, at Hajar, also in that country. Its greatest length is two hundred and eighty feet; the wall at its highest point is thirty-five

butable to a people probably from Libya in Africa, who settled in Sardinia. They say (p. 13) that it is in accordance with all probability that the nearest continent should furnish Sardinia with its first inhabitants. Hisorical and geographical nomenclature recalls that of Africa (Pais, "La Sardegna," p. 16). Pausanias tells us (x., xvii. 4), "It is said that it is Libyans who were the first to pass into that island." Several other theories are discussed, but the arguments in favour of the Libyans are declared to be the best. We are told: "They crossed with their wives and children in great boats similar to those in which they had so hardily engaged in the mouths of the river and in the canals of Lower Egypt." The monuments of Phœnician worship are no doubt to be found in the Sardinian Nauraghe ruins—both monoliths and stones with most unmistakable emblems. In the absence of historical narratives great room for conjecture exists as to when and how this worship was practised by the ancient inhabitants of Sardinia, who built the fortresses and other buildings whose consideration has already tasked the energies and elicited the divergent opinions of archæologists. Among the authors quoted by Perrot and Chipiez feet above the ground, and fifteen feet at the lowest; its greatest base thickness is sixteen feet two inches, and its thinnest point is about five feet. . . . There are three entrances to this circular building. The principal one, only three feet wide, faces the hill fortress and the north. . . . The great and astounding feature is the long narrow passage leading

are Pausanias, x., xvii.; Niebuhr, "Romische Geschichte;" Maury, "La Terre et l'Homme," 4me edition; D'Arbois de Jubainville, "Les Anciens Habitants de l'Europe;" Renan, "Histoire générale des langues semetiques," 4me edition; "La Revue Archæologique," tome xvi.; Chabas, "Recherches;" Lieblein, "Notices sur les monuments Egyptiens trouvés en Sardaigne," Christiana, 1879; "Bulletins Archæologia Sardo," 1884; Pais, "La Sardegna;" M. Maspero, "Histoire ancienne des peuples de l'Orient;" Duncker, "Geschichte des Alterthums;" M. Halevy, "Études Berberes dans le Journal Asiatique," 1874, tome ix.; Lenormant, "Histoire ancienne des peuples de l'Orient," 9e edition, tome ii.; La Marmora, "Voyage en Sardaigne;" M. Gouin, "Notice sur les Mines de l'Ile de Sardaigne," Cagliari, 1867; Diodorus, iv., xxx., 1; Olio y Quadrado, "Historia de la Isla de Minorca," 1876. F. Lenormant, "Notes archæologiques sur les terre d'Otrante, dans la Gazette Archæologique," 7^e annee; Aristotle, iv., xi., 1; Alexandre Bertrand, "L'Allee couvertes de Conflans et les Dolmans troues" ("Archæologie celtique et gauloise, 1876").

direct from the main entrance to the sacred enclosure, so narrow in parts that two people cannot walk abreast, whilst on either side of you rise the stupendous walls, thirty feet in height, and built with such evenness of courses and symmetry that as a specimen of the dry builders' art it is without parallel. . . . The actual approaches to the sacred enclosure are most carefully defended with buttresses on either side, into which a form of portcullis has been fixed. A monolith rose from a raised platform in front of a large round tower (there are the remains of two round towers in the centre of the enclosure). "The religious purport of these towers would seem to be conclusively proved by the numerous finds we made in the ruins of a phallic nature, and I think a quotation from Montfaucon's 'L'Antiquité Expliquée' will give us the key-note of the worship. The ancients assure us that all the Arabians worship a tower, which they called El Acara, or Alquetila, which was built by their Patriarch Ishmael." *

* "Ruined Cities of Mashonaland," *ut supra*. It has been deemed wise to treat the temple buildings in an entirely separate manner, as it is evident that their nature, character, and object are distinct.

"Maximus of Tyre says they honoured as a great god a great cut stone*; this is apparently the same stone resembling Venus, according to Euthymius Zygabenus. This tower doubtless corresponded to the sacred tower of the Midianites, called Penuel, or the 'Face of God,' which Gideon destroyed (Judges viii. 7). Turning to Phœnician temple construction, we have a good parallel to the ruins of the great Zimbabwe at Byblos, as depicted on the coins. The tower or sacred cone is set up within the temple precincts and shut off in an enclosure." Mr. Bent then goes on to refer to ancient buildings of the same class at Malta and other places, concluding the reference by saying, "Hence it would

---

* The reader's special attention is called to the important passage quoted from Mr. Bent's work. There can be little doubt but that the very early Nature worshippers who adopted the Phœnician Nature religion were stone worshippers. This fact, it will be seen, will help us in the sequel to fix to some extent the period when the Zimbabwe forts, &c., were built. On the subject of the stone worship of the ancients see very learned and able treatises by F. Lenormant, "Les Betyles" and "Sol Elagabalus," published in "La Revue de l'Histoire des Religions, Deuxieme Année," Paris, 1881.

appear that the same influence was at work in Sardinia as in South Africa."*

Now, turning to Sardinia, we find that circles of stones exist near the forts, as in South-east Africa. They are styled by the people the "Tombs of the Giants," where they have found human bones accompanied by arms of bronze and large vessels of copper. These tombs were all oriented so that the first

---

* Bent's "Ruined Cities of Mashonaland," p. 100. A learned and interesting chapter (v. p. 120) is supplied to this work by Mr. R. W. Swan, in which he treats "Of the Orientation and Measurement of the Zimbabwe Ruins." He tells us that the most important feature in the interior of the temple is of course the great tower. "The only interesting mathematical fact which seems to have been embodied in the architecture of the temples is the ratio of diameter to circumference, and it may have had an occult significance in the peculiar form of Nature worship which was practised there." At the highest point of the eminence is erected the great monolith, which seems to have marked the meridian for the altar. He says that the balance of probabilities seems to be in favour of the opinion that the builders of the great Zimbabwe came from South Arabia, and he speaks of the similarity of ruins in Yemen to those in South-east Africa. Mr. Swan makes elaborate calculations with reference to possible Sun and Star worship at Zimbabwe, and ends by saying that "There are many astronomical points in these buildings to be yet considered."

rays of the rising sun in summer would shine upon them.* The authors of the great French history of Art (Perrot and Chipiez) inform us that the builders of the Nauraghes and the tombs were the same people, and they refer to the mistaken ideas concerning them expressed by Aristotle and his contemporaries. They add that the Sardinian tomb is indeed nothing but a development or a completion of Megalithic monuments such as those found in India, Palestine, and North Africa.† The pictures given as illustrative of the nature and character of these interesting remains are well worthy of study. Besides these, it is important to know that circles of stones

* See La Marmora, "Voyage," ii. p. 34. The plates in his Atlas have been copied by Perrot and Chipiez in their "Histoire de l'Art," tome iv. p. 55, *et seq*.

† On p. 60 Perrot and Chipiez refer to the conical stones, well worked, found in Sardinia, but not to their knowledge in the Balearic Isles. In subsequent pages they refer to the distinct phallic representations found engraved on stones, and to the great raised stones, both of which prove almost an exact similitude between the worship of the builders of the Nauraghes and "Tombs of the Giants" in Sardinia and the people who erected the Zimbabwes in South-east Africa. See Perrot and Chipiez, "Histoire de l'Art," tome iv. p. 63.

are not rare in the island. They are more often of an elliptic than circular form, and their greatest diameter is from twelve to fifteen metres. At one place another and smaller circle has been formed at a short distance, and there are in it and on an eminence two dressed stones, while it is noticeable that the place of the raised stones seems to indicate the entrance. "It is in the same territory that on blocks of 'trachyte' are sculptured the phallus in bas-relief."

The following conclusions seem to arise from the preceding:—First, the builders of the Zimbabwes in South-east Africa and of the Nauraghes in Sardinia were Nature worshippers of the early Phœnician cult, when stone worship was one of the leading features of that religion. Second, the arguments of MM. Perrot and Chipiez point to the fact that the Nauraghe builders came from Libya, and we shall see in due course that the intermixture of the African and Arabian peoples was of a peculiar and intimate character. Third, we may venture to attribute a very remote antiquity (the Bronze Age) to both classes of buildings: certainly we can scarcely be wrong in concluding that the oldest of the Zimbabwes of South-eastern Africa were erected before the ninth century B.C. There is little doubt that some of them existed when Hiram, King of Tyre, obtained gold for the Temple of Solomon, and we shall see in the sequel that ancient Monomotapa was probably one of the Ophirs * referred to in the Sacred Scriptures.

One of the most primitive forms of idolatrous religions is litholatry. The great archæologist, Lenormant,† tells us that " in the first ages an unformed 'dressed' stone was one of the objects which served to represent the divinity and offer a sensible sign for adoration." This was specially a form of the early Phœnician religion, which some writers tell us was possibly in the first place monotheistic, but developed into a pantheistical personification of the forces of nature. It

---

* "Ophir" was a generic title for a rich commercial country used in the same way as "Tarshish." The latter name we know was given to more than one place, so there may have been an Indian as well as an African Ophir. The former would be on the Malabar coast; the latter was inland from the Sofala coast, in South-east Africa (Monomotapa).

† "Revue de l'Histoire des Religions," tome iii. p. 31.

represented the male and female principles of production, and in its later and popular forms became a worship of the sun, moon, and planets. Nothing more corrupt, debasing, and cruel than this religion in remote antiquity

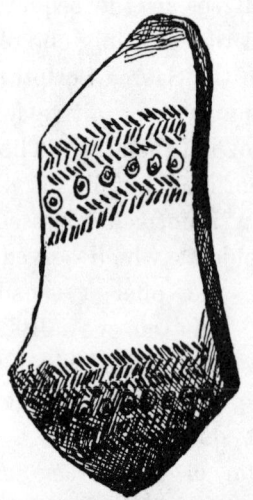

FIG. 11. FORM OF VASE.
(*From Baux.*)

can be imagined, and a study of its ceremonies and practices explains to some extent the awful denunciations hurled against the followers of Baal in the Old Testament. Stones of the conic description symbolised sometimes a male god, as in the case of Jupiter Meilichios of Sicyon, which appeared to have been originally a Phœnician Moloch, the Apollos of Epirus, Megira, and of Aptera in Crete. These idols were formed after the Syrian model, as that of Bel in the great temple of Palmyra, which was the same as the Phœnician Baal Hamman referred to in the Sanchoniathon of Philo of Byblos. Sometimes female goddesses were represented by blocks of stone, as in the cases of Aphrodite at Cyprus, and of Tanith in Carthage. These latter goddesses were evidently of Phœnician origin. We are told that upon coins of the isle of Ceos the figures of Jupiter and Juno are represented by two conical pillars. This veneration for conical stones was sometimes exhibited in relation to natural rocks which presented this form, as in the case of two rocks which rise out of the sea near Tyre. In the Syro-Phœnician religion the worship of the conical stone was closely allied to that of the mountain, of which it was a diminutive. Herodotus informs us * that rectangular dressed stones, used as representatives of deities, were

* Herodotus, bk. iii. p. 8.

very much multiplied among the Arabs. Maximin of Tyre* and Clement of Alexandria † give us the same information. Porphyry says,‡ "The Arabs of Duma each year sacrificed an infant and interred it at the foot of the stone which served as a divine image." In an old Arab verse § are the words: "I have sworn by the blood which flows upon Auzh and upon the sacred stones (ancâb) which surround Soûair." In the Phœnician religion "The Necib" corresponds to the word "nocb" among Arabian idolaters, and we are told that the Phœnician stones, whose inscriptions commenced by the expression "necib Malik Baal" formed a usual form of dedication. Certain rocks were adored by the Arabs simply because they naturally reproduced the form of a raised parallelogramatic form,‖ and we have abundant evidence

* Dissertation, viii. 8.

† Protept. iv. 46.

‡ De abstin. carn. ii. p. 203.

§ Diwan I. 5, p. 35; *Journ. Asiat.*, 6th series, vol. xii. pp. 270 and 305.

‖ Studied with attention, the Old Testament history referring to Jacob throws a curious light on the ancient stone worship. Jacob arrives at night in a place of of the worship in hundreds of votive stones whose inscriptions in Himyaritic characters, discovered chiefly in Southern Arabia, can now be consulted in the British Museum. In the Vatican Library we have had the privilege of referring to large numbers of beautiful photographs of votive stones found in Arabia,*

great stones which were venerated. He sleeps with one of these as his pillow, and he enjoys a wonderful dream. The place is called *Bethel* (the House of God), but it is argued that the word is derived from *Betúli Baitulia,* or sacred stones. Of course the idolaters honoured the stones not merely as the dwelling-place of God (Hebrew *bethêl*, Phœnician *bêthül*, Syriac *baitô aloho*), but even as God Himself. This notion of a divinity resident in a stone, sometimes fashioned partially by man's hand, became in a particular fashion attached to aerolites, such as the black stone (Kaabah) of Mecca is believed to be. Such was the stone adored upon Ida, and that famous one at Emesus, styled "Elagabalus." On coins of Sulpicius Antoninus and Heliogabalus this is merely figured as a conical stone. The famous stone of Delphos was considered to be the one given to Chronos by Rhea in order to save Jupiter. We are told that the employment of the aerolite (Betylus) as a divine image, although certainly Hellenic, had its root in the Phœnician religion.

* See "Corpus Inscriptionum Semiticarum ab Academia Inscriptionum et literam humaniorum conditum atque digestum—Pars Prima. Inscriptiones Phœnicias continens," Paris, 1881. Here there is a magnificent

42   MONOMOTAPA.

with such inscriptions as the following—thus
rendered into Latin:—

> Dominæ Tanith faciei
> Baal et Domus Baal
> Hamman : quod vovit
> Bad Melkart, filiŭs
> Baal Itan, filii
> Hanna.

A consideration of the Phœnician religion

series of excellent photographs of the inscriptions on
votive stones found in Arabia, of which the Latin translation in the text is a fair specimen. On the subject of
the stone worship of the Phœnicians, Arabians, and
others, the following works can be consulted :—François
Lenormant, "Les Betyles en Revue de l'histoire des
Religions," tome troisieme, p. 31; C. P. Tiele, in the
same volume, "La Religion Phœnicienne," p. 167; F.
Lenormant, in the same volume, "Sol Elagabalus," p.
310 ; " Dictionnaire des Antiquités Grecques et Romains"
—article Bætylia ; Maury, "Histoire des Religions de
la Grece," t. i. p. 180, *et suiv*; Girard de Rialle, "Mythologie comparee," t. i. pp. 13–30; Pausanias, ix., 22,
24, 27 ; Lucretius, "De natura rerum," V. v. 1198;
Ovid, "Fasta," II. v. 64 ; Tibullus, i. 1, v. 11.; Pro-
pertius, i. 4, v. 23 ; Lucian, "De dea Syria," 16 ;
Baettiger, "Ideen zur kunst Mythologie"; Clermont-
Ganneau, *Journal Asiatique*, 7ᵉ série, t. x. p. 221 ; Eck-
hel, "Catali Musei Vindobonensis," t. i. p. 102 ; Mionnet,
"Description des Medailles ; antiques Supplement," tome
iii. p. 318 ; Combe, "Meseum Hunterianum," pl. iv., No.

takes us to prehistoric times and to the most ancient records of the world. There is reason

6; Muller, "Wieseler Denkmaeler der alten kunst," t. 1, pl. 1, No. 2; Milligan, "Ancient Coins," pl. iii., No. 19; "Voy. de vogue Syrie central, Inscriptions semitiques," p. 85; Gesenius, "Monumenta Phœnicia," pl. xxiii., No. 60; "Sanchoniathon," p. 6, ed. Orelli; Gesenius, "Thesaurus," v.; Gerhard, "Gesammelte akademische Abhandlungen," pl. xli. No. 2; Lajard, "Culte de Venus," pl. 1, Nos. 10 to 12; F. Lenormant, "Monographie de la voie Sacré Eleusinienne," t. i. p. 360–2; Hamaker, "Diatribe philologo-critica monumentorum aliquot punicorum nuper in Africa," &c., pl. i. Nos. 1 to 4; "La Marmora Nouv.-ann. de l'Institut Archæologique," t. i. p. 10, *et suiv*; Fr. Lenormant, "Origines de l'Histoire," t. i. p. 539; Movers, "Die Phœnizier," t. i. p. 657; Gerhard, "Antike Bildwertke"; Melin, "Galerie mythologique"; Pococke, "Spec-hist. Arab." Note sur les pierres sacrées appelees en phenicien "necib malac baal," *Journal Asiatique*, 7e série, t. viii.; Caussin de Perceval, "Histoire des Arabes," t. i. p. 242; Falconnet, "Dissertation sur les Batyles dans les Mémoires de l'Academie des Inscriptions," tome vi.; Munter, "Ueber die von Himmel gefallene Steine," Copenhagen, 1805; Baettiger, "Ideen zu kunst mythologie," t. ii. p. 15–18; D. De Luynes, "Numismatiques et Inscriptions Cypriotes," pl. vii., Nos. 3 and 4. These are among the works aptly quoted by Lenormant in the dissertation on Litholatry which we have followed. Ed. Glaeser, in his works published under the auspices of the Academy of Inscriptions, refers to the great ruins which he found on a hill in Arabia. These were formed of large rude stones, and to believe that these people may originally have been Monotheists. Certainly they considered that the Creator was wholly distinct from matter, and brought into existence all other beings and all material things.* But this belief was corrupted at a very early period, and as Lucifer fell from heaven so did this monotheistic belief descend into the depths of litholatry, licentiousness, and the

---

seem identical in character with those of the Zimbabwes of South-east Africa. We can also refer our readers to Hartwig Durembourg, "Les Manuscrits Arabes de l'Escurial," Paris, 1884; Halevy Joseph, "Rapport sur un Mission archæologique dans le Yemen"; Abu Mohammed Al Hasan ibn Ahmad ibn Yakub ibn Jusup ibn David, in the year of the Hegira 334 (of Christ 945), wrote two great works on Arabia Felix, referred to by A. von Kremer in his "Culturgeschichte des Orients unter den Chalifen" (Wein, 1875). It is clear, on a full consideration of the question, that those who erected the Nauraghes in Sardinia, as well as the builders of ancient monuments where votive stones have been found, as in Yemen (Arabia), and also the people who made originally the Zimbabwes in South-east Africa, all practised the same early form of the Phœnician Nature worship manifested in litholatry. In the sequel we will endeavour to show that the period in which these people lived was previous to the tenth century before Christ.

* See "Phœnicia," by Prof. Geo. Rawlinson, in the series of Stories of the Nations, p. 29.

most abandoned cruelty. To refer in any clear, consecutive, and precise manner to the early nature and progress of this religion is impossible. Indeed, it is now an ascertained fact that it is in vain to seek for materials upon which to found a description of the primitive Phœnician religion.* Merged with the Canaanites, the Phœnicians eventually came forth a separate people. A great authority says, "With the documents which we possess it is yet impossible to write a history of the religion of the Phœnicians." "All that it is possible to do is to determine and to characterise the elements which enter into its formation, and to classify them after an approximate chronological order." † In the first epoch we find the worship of the Goddess of Fertility (mother of the gods) and of her young spouse Adonis. This was

---

* See C. P. Tiele in his article, "La Religion des Phenicians," in "La Revue de l'Histoire des Religions," tome iii. p. 171, on the subject of the complete unreliability of the earliest records—specially including the fables (Cosmogony) furnished by Philo of Byblos in his asserted work of Sanchoniathon—extracts of which have come down to us preserved by Eusebius and Porphyry.

† Ibid., p. 172.

intimately connected in character with the Greek worship of Chronos, and is the Canaaneo-Syrian element in all its purity. Then came the great gods of Sidon, and in these two periods the conic stone and other representations of the powers of nature held a prominent place.* In this second period Sidon

---

* The Orphic fragments contain what may be styled the remotest fragments of Greek sacerdotal philosophy. According to this authority all the departments of nature were animated by living powers which are portions of the supreme or universal Soul into whose essence all finite beings are resolved. This Pantheistic system kept really no hold on the world, and degenerated into vicious and cruel heathenism. Proclus proclaims the ancient Phœnician religion when he says (liber v.), "Cælam et Terram quasi male et feminam respicere licet. Est enim Cæli motus qui ex diurna revelutione viret seminales edit unde Terra quæ eminant respecit." The mysteries of Eleusis and of Samothrace were no doubt connected with this Nature worship. C. P. Tiele tells us in "La Religion Phœnicienne," already quoted (p. 196), "The most ancient religion of Syria, of Phœnicia, and of Canaan consisted in the fundamental idea of the fruitful marriage of heaven with earth, or the vivifying mysterious action of fire in the waters of the celestial ocean." Conical stones, and even huge rough blocks of stone, became the expressions of this religion—in an idol form. Columns of stone were consecrated to Baal Hamman (referred to in the Old Testament) in Canaan. In the great temple of

attained its greatest power, commencing in the sixteenth century B.C. and terminating about the twelfth century B.C., probably at the epoch of the sack of Sidon by the Philistines. The principal Sidonian families took refuge at Tyre, and there formed a monarchical and aristocratic power. The religion of the second great city differed little from that of the first. The worship of Ashtaroth lost a little of its importance when Baal-Melgart of Tyre and Eshmoun of Sidon became the popular gods. The reign of Hiram was the culminating point of the glory

Tyre, constructed by Hiram, these columns were of jasper; in that of Cadiz, in Spain, the columns were of copper. The two columns or pillars of the Temple of Solomon were styled Yakin and Boaz. No images of gods existed in Tyre in Hiram's time—only columns or blocks of stone. At our Zimbabwes in South-east Africa no images of gods—no idols, indeed, except blocks of stone—have been discovered. This seems to give some indication of the early period when the forts, &c., were built. Of course, roughly-hewn images of birds have been found, but these were scarcely idols. We find that the vulture was the *totem* of an Arabian tribe at the time of the Himyaritic ascendency. Mr. Bent justly considers ("Ruined Cities of Mashonaland," p. 155) that this is a link between South-east African Zimbabwe builders and the people of Saba.

and power of the great city of Tyre. Temples of Baal were magnificently restored, and in one of them he placed the celebrated column of gold which became the admiration of the heathen world. In the ninth century before Christ the Phœnician religion began to decline, and is emphatically declared "to have no longer a history." Although flourishing in Carthage it languished in its original home, and soon became merged in the various heathen superstitions of the world. The great period of litholatry permeating heathenism probably animated the centuries which preceded and attended the great era of Phœnician prosperity when Hiram, King of Tyre, traded through Arabia to the Ophirs of India and Africa. If this be so the builders of the Zimbabwes erected the first of their edifices before Solomon reigned in Jerusalem, when the maledictions of God were hurled against the worship of stones in the "high places in Palestine," and at a time when licentious rites disgraced the name of man in Canaan. With Polytheism naturally came the degradation of the divine idea. Baal was identified with the Sun; Ishtar, or

Ashtaroth, with the Moon; and not only did Nature worship give rise to the most licentious orgies, but even to frequent and extensive massacres of human beings.

The history of the people of Phœnicia, to whom we trace the litholatry exhibited in ancient monuments on the shores of the Mediterranean, in the fertile country of Arabia, and amidst the ancient gold mines of South-eastern Africa, is a study of absorbing interest. What the Great British Empire is to the nineteenth century Phœnicia was to the distant ages when Solomon's Temple was built at Jerusalem, and Hiram, King of Tyre, sent out expeditions to the distant shores of India, Arabia, and South-eastern Africa.

The question of the Latin poet Ovid, "What land hath not known, what sea hath not heard, of Arion?" was applicable to the nation whose scanty tract of country—"Palmland"—extended for a distance of two hundred miles along the Eastern Mediterranean, from a little below the thirty-third to a little below the thirty-sixth parallel of north latitude. It has been well said that size is an insignificant element in rating a country's position, as witness, Sparta, Athens, Carthage, Genoa, and Venice; while in more recent times Portugal, Holland, and England have accentuated the fact. Certain it is that from the little territory of Phœnicia came forth the most skilful and the most daring mariners of ancient times. No terrors of unknown seas * nor distant lands daunted them, and we consequently find that not merely did they permeate the Mediterranean, but they advanced through the pillars of Hercules to the coast of Britain, and at the same time went south to India, to Arabia,

* "Without any doubt the successful Phœnician mariners underwent both severe hardship and great real perils, beside those still greater supposed perils, the apprehension of which so constantly unnerved the minds of even experienced and resolute men in the unknown ocean. Such was the force of these terrors and difficulties to which there was no known termination upon the mind of the Archemenid Sataspes (upon whom the navigation of Africa was imposed as a penalty 'worse than death,' by Xerxes, in commutation of a capital sentence) that he returned without having finished the circuit, though by doing so he forfeited his life" (Grote's "History of Greece," vol. ii. p. 462). Professor Rawlinson adds to this, "The Phœnicians were braver; they persevered, and by so doing added another leaf to the unfading laurel crown which the voice of history awards them for their daring and intrepidity."

and to the still more distant shores of Sofala. Indeed there is little doubt that they circumnavigated Africa according to the account of Herodotus, and there is some reason to believe that in these remote ages whose records never existed, or are completely lost in the mists of antiquity, they may have found the great western continent and planted a civilisation there whose only remains are the enigmatic colossal monuments of bygone races of the world.

In an interview with Mr. George Dennis, the well-known archæologist, in Rome, that gentleman informed us that many years ago, when in Demerara (British Guiana), he became aware of the fact that a number of very ancient inscribed stones were in existence on the property of a planter with whom he was acquainted. An exact copy of the inscription on one of these was sent to Dr. S. Birch, then Curator of Oriental Antiquities in the British Museum, who stated in his reply that he could not recognise any Punic words, but acknowledged the general resemblance of the characters to Punic letters. In a lecture "On the Aborigines of South America and Speculations on their Origin," by George Dennis, C.M.G., D.C.L., delivered before the Archæological Society of Rome (Session 1892–1893) we are told, "If these rock-cut characters be really Punic, they prove that in very early times some Phœnician or Carthaginian vessel must have visited these shores. In no case can such inscriptions be attributed to the Aborigines, who, before their intercourse with Europeans, had no knowledge of metals, still less of letters, or of representing objects in nature. . . . The Phœnicians, the most adventurous sailors and explorers of antiquity, as well as the most enterprising traders, who made settlements outside the Pillars of Hercules, and who certainly discovered the various islands of the North-west Coast of Africa—' The Islands of the Blessed '—these adventurers, when in the latitude of the trade winds, may have been tempted to avail themselves of these steady breezes to explore the oceans of the West in search of new marts. . . . What more probable than that traces of such a visit should be found on the North-eastern Coast of South America, the nearest portion of that continent to the old world, while all record of the discovery of a new continent has been lost?" The distance was not great, *viâ* the Isthmus of Panama, to these provinces, whose ancient Aztec civilisation is buried in mystery. Recent writers of authority inform us that in the colossal ruins of Mexico there are evident traces of Chaldæan workmanship, and we know that the Phœnicians were closely allied in language and religion to that nation. Mr. Owen Jones, in his "Grammar of Ornament," refers to the "fret" used as a decoration among the Greeks, and by the original inhabitants of Yucatan. Mr. Dennis (lecture already quoted) is confident that there was intercourse in very early prehistoric times between the natives of the American continent and the nations of the old world. Among other evidence he refers to rude characters and ruder figures of men and boats of archaic forms found upon smooth rocks at the foot of the falls of the Essequiba river.

The Geographical Society of California has published a

pamphlet, written by Mr. Thomas Crawford Johnston, entitled, "Did the Phœnicians discover America?" The question is answered in the affirmative, and the reasons for this reply are both numerous and ingenious. "Masonry of the most massive character has been found on various islands of the Pacific, resembling the still extant substructions of Solomon's Temple, which we know were the work of Hiram, King of Tyre." Chief among these are the ruins on Easter Island. "A high civilisation having an identical origin must, at some remote period, have prevailed throughout Polynesia." Mr. Johnston believes that the Phœnicians approached America from the West, going, in the first instance, down the Red Sea, *viâ* Hindostan and Ceylon—and thence *viâ* Sumatra and Java to the Caroline Islands, Tonga, Samoa, &c., thence to Peru and Mexico. It is contended that the form of religious worship which Cortez found existing in Mexico was clearly Phœnician in its base and entire outline. "The human sacrifice and the idol half man and half brute are beyond question those of the Phœnician Baal or Moloch; while on various bronzes we see the winged disc of Egypt, one of the peculiar designs of the Phœnicians. . . . Baal became identified with the Sun and Ashtaroth with the Moon, and a general belief prevailed that the anger of the gods was best averted by human sacrifices. Not only in Phœnicia proper, but throughout its entire colonial system there was an established practice of offering up human sacrifices, especially in times of public calamity. . . . In the Pacific we find traces of this belief spread from shore to shore. . . . Among the early inhabitants of Mexico human sacrifice prevailed to an alarming extent. . . . Their deity under another name corresponded with the Phœnician Baal or

Moloch. . . . Among the Chinchemees we find the old and distinctly Phœnician custom of an open-air worship of the Sun and Moon, and the strange custom of presenting to the Sun the bleeding heart torn from the victim before throwing it with the rest of the carcase at the feet of the image to be consumed with fire." Mr. Dennis truly says that the line of argument advanced by Mr. Johnston is to prove that the Aztec civilisation was the product of Phœnician adventure. Prescott, in his "History of the Conquest of Mexico," informs us that Hernan Cortez was informed that the tradition of the people themselves was in favour of their fathers having come from a distant land in the North-west. As the original people of the Pacific Islands and America are declared to be Mongolians, who were assisted in their migration from the East or North-east Coast of Asia by the Aleutian Islands, it is clear that if they did discover and visit America and the islands of the Pacific, they were merely foreigners who became merged in the population without changing the physical character of the people, although they may have largely influenced their customs and religion; these speculations clearly show how much the very distant voyages of the Phœnicians are supposed to have affected the earliest known nations of the world.

About 2,000 years before Christ Semitic emigrants advanced into the coast tract extending from the borders of Egypt to the deep valley of the Jordan and soon became masters of the Hamite tribes who had previously settled there. The men who conquered the Canaanites and Philistines were Hebrews, Phœnicians, and Syrians. The whole history of the ancient world is specially marked by the records of mighty migrations, and one of the earliest of these comprised the great wave of Semitic nations which poured from the lands of the Euphrates to the shores of the Mediterranean. In this were the Phœnician people who came from Arabia.* This exodus took place before the Israelites quitted Egypt, at least if there be some uncertainty about this statement there does not seem to be any doubt that from the fourteenth to the fourth century before Christ the Phœnicians occupied the small tract of

---

* Herodotus informs us that the Phœnicians, in their own account of themselves, stated that many years before the siege of Troy they came from the Persian Gulf to Syria. Justin tells us that the Tyrian nation was founded by the Phœnicians, who, being disturbed by an earthquake, moved viâ Assyria to their new homes; and Renan says that "The greater number of modern critics admit it as demonstrated that the primitive abode of the Phœnicians must be placed on the Lower Euphrates, in the centre of the great commercial and maritime establishments of the Persian Gulf conformably to the unanimous witness of antiquity" (Renan, "Histoire des langues semitiques," ii., 2, p. 183). See Professor Rawlinson, "Phœnicia," pp. 21, 22.

Mediterranean coast which bore their name, whence they sent forward the most daring and successful fleets and colonies of antiquity. No people of the ancient world had so much to do with Britain and with Ireland, while their sails traversed not merely the Mediterranean and the North Atlantic, but even the far shores of the Erythræan sea and the still more distant coasts of Africa. For one thousand years they were the premier explorers, merchants, and navigators of the world. Not only were they the greatest traders, but incomparably the foremost miners * and metallurgists

---

* Strabo and Pliny tell us (Strabo, xiv. 5, § 28 ; Pliny, H. N., vii., 56) that the Phœnicians passed to the Thracian mainland and worked the gold mines of Mount Pangæus in the vicinity of Philippi. We know that the British tin mines worked by the Phœnicians were remarkably rich—so valuable, indeed, that Strabo tells us of a case where a Tyrian captain, followed by a Roman ship when near the Cassiterides, preferred to run his ship upon the rocks rather than allow a rival nation to learn the secret of the safe approach to the tin-producing coast. The first extensive mining operations of the Phœnicians were probably commenced at Cyprus, where Pliny informs us (Pliny, H. N., xxxv., 2), "In Cypro prima aeris inventio." However, the earliest mining operations of which we have any record were conducted by Egyptian kings of the fourth, fifth, and

PHŒNICIA.

of their time. Their rich mines in Spain, Britain, and Cyprus only stimulated their exertions in other parts of the world. They were not merely traders, but explorers and colonists. Their small territory required outlets for a redundant population, and these were found in various parts of the known and unknown world. A policy of profound secretiveness retained as much as possible the knowledge of some of those Tarshishes and Ophirs of which they were the discoverers. They went everywhere and were successful where-

twelfth dynasties in the region extending between Suez and Mount Sinai. Their shafts were laboriously excavated in the rocks (see Brugsch, "History of Egypt," i., 65. Deuteronomy viii., 7, 9). It is believed that the Phœnicians learnt mining from the Egyptians, and finding that their own territories supplied them very scantily with metals, sent out expeditions constantly in search of lands where they could obtain valuable mines. Sardinia was certainly occupied by Phœnicians, or people of Phœnician religion, who worked rich mines of copper and lead in the south-western portion of the island (see Rawlinson, "History of Phœnicia," p. 313). In Spain, however, was one of the richest of the Tarshishes of the world, where silver was found in great abundance. We are told that the methods used to obtain the metals were not dissimilar to those now employed. They are thus described : " Where the metal (gold) lay deeper than the ever they went. In all history there is no greater analogy than that between the Empire of Britain in the nineteenth century and that of Phœnicia at its culminating point of glory, six hundred years before the birth of our Saviour.

The principal carrying trade of the world was performed by the Phœnicians. No state of antiquity understood the art of successful colonisation so well, and none was more

surface, perpendicular shafts were sunk into the ground, sometimes, if we may believe Diodorus (Diod. Sic., v., 34, § 2) to the depth of half a mile or more; from these shafts horizontal adits were carried out at various levels, and from the adits there branched lateral galleries, sometimes at right angles, sometimes obliquely, which pursued either a straight or a tortuous course (Και πλαγίας σκολίας δίαδυσεις ποικλίως μεταλουργουντες). The veins of the metal were perseveringly followed up, and where faults occurred in them filled with hard rock (see Pliny, H. N., xxxiii., 4, § 71; also §§ 70, 73) the obstacle was either tunnelled through or its flank turned." Roofs were arched or supported with wooden posts. Galleries were frequently driven into the mountain side to procure metallic ores—and in all mines when water was troublesome draining tunnels were attempted when possible, but there was no means of pumping water from a mine. The invention of the Archimedes screw did not take place until B.C. 220–190. On this mining subject we have followed Rawlinson, " Phœnicia," pp. 316, 317.

fortunate in the choice of those whom she used both for mining and commercial purposes. Her manufactures were the most excellent and the most valued in these times, and her trade both by land and sea had no rival. From each colony special commodities were procured which were taken in return for her own manufactures of linen, wool, cotton, silk, pottery, metals, and glass. With uncivilised nations large profits were obtained by giving them clothes, utensils, and ornaments at lower rates than those charged by the native artisan, whose products were driven out of the market to find room for those from the marts of Phœnicia. It is idle to name countries which were traded with when the whole world seems to have been the theatre of her explorations and colonising schemes. There is every probability that, according to Herodotus, Phœnician mariners explored the coast of Libya beyond the Red Sea in the seventh century before Christ, and eventually returned home by the pillars of Hercules.*

---

* Herodotus, iv. 1. Professor Rawlinson says, "What so sceptical a writer as Mr. Grote admits and accepts will scarcely be rejected by the more candid criticism

This was the great dominating commercial power whose traffic and riches are frequently referred to by various writers in the Old Testament.* How glorious was the position

of the present day. . . . The reality of this circumnavigation and the general credibility of the narrative have been the object of much doubt and criticism. But there seems to be no reason why the physical difficulties should not have been overcome by a people accustomed to confront the dangers of the open Atlantic. . . . The principal argument in favour of the actual circumnavigation having been effected lies in the story told by the mariners on their return, which Herodotus discredited. They said that in sailing round South Africa they had after a time the sun on their right hand. It was a phenomenon not within the cognisance of any Greek nor probably of any Phœnician or Egyptian. Their tale was incredible to their contemporaries and to many succeeding generations of men. . . . But the fact of their making the report is evidence to us of their having actually experienced the phenomena. This feat is one that deserves to be recorded in any history which treats of the Phœnicians. It is doubtful whether the enterprise was ever repeated until nearly the close of the fifteenth century, when Vasco da Gama revolutionised the commerce of the world by doubling the Cape from the West" (Rawlinson, "History of Phœnicia," p. 179).

* "Tyre heaped up silver as the dust and fine gold as the mire of the streets" (Zechariah ix. 3). "Arabia and all the princes of Kedar they occupied with thee in lambs, and rams and goats: in these were they thy merchants.

described by the Prophet Ezekiel when he declares (Ezek. xxvii.):

> "Thus said the Lord God, thou O Tyre, hast said I am
>   perfect in beauty.
> Thy borders are in the heart of the Sea;
> Thy builders have perfected thy beauty.
> They have made all thy planks of fir trees from Senir;
> They have taken cedars from Lebanon to make a mast
>   for thee,
> Of the oaks of Bashan have they made thine oars;
> They have made thy benches of ivory,
> Inlaid in boxwood from the isles of Kittim.
>
> .   .   .   .   .
>
> All the ships of the sea with their mariners were in
>   thee
> That they might occupy thy merchandise.
> Persia and Lud and Phut were in thy army, thy men
>   of war;
> They hanged the shield and helmet in thee—

The merchants of Sheba and Ramaah, they were thy merchants: they occupied in thy fairs with chief of all spices and with all precious stones and gold" (Ezek. xxvii. 21, 22). See as to the trade with Tyre, Ezek. xxvii. 13; buying of captives sold into slavery, Joel iii. 6; constant supply of slaves, Ezek. xxvii. 13; Babylonia and Assyria supplied Phœnicia with embroidery of great value, Ezek. xxvii. 23, 24; their trade in beasts of burthen, Ezek. xxvii. 14, 1 Kings i. 33; cloths for chariots, coverings of tents, ivory, ebony, wrought iron, Ezek. xxvii. 20, xxvi. 7, 14, xxvii. 15, 19–22; Esther viii. 10, 14.

Tarshish was thy merchant by reason of the multitude
of all kinds of riches—
With silver, iron, tin, and lead, they traded for thy
wares.

. . . . . .

Arabia and all the merchants of Kedar they were the
merchants of thy hand;
In lambs and rams and goats, in these were thy
merchants,
The traffickers of Sheba and Raamah, they were thy
traffickers;
They traded for thy wares with chief of all spices,
And with all manner of precious stones and gold.
Haran, and Cannah and Eden, the traffickers of Sheba,
Asshur and Chilmad, were thy traffickers."

The history of Phœnicia is in so many respects composed merely of reasonable conjectures that the materials for a connected narrative can scarcely be said to exist.*

* Sanchoniathon's so-called history is looked upon with suspicion. It comprises a cosmogony said to be written by Philo of Byblus, and only fragments of the work have been preserved in the pages of Eusebius and Porphyry. Undoubtedly many Phœnician works have perished. Moschus of Sidon wrote upon the doctrine of the formation of the world from atoms. Josephus cites "Annals of the Town of Tyre." A History of Tyre was written by Menander of Ephesus, but has not come down to our time. The following are some of the books which may be referred to with advantage:—" De Fœnicum

Certain it is that these people spoke a Semitic language closely akin to that of the Hebrew,*

literis," J. Postell, Paris, 1552; Sanchoniathon's "Phœnician History," translated, London, 1720; "Reflexions sur quelques monuments," &c., Abbé Barthelemy, Paris, 1739; "De Alfuteta y lingua de los Phenices e de sus Colonias," J. Ibarra, Madrid, 1772; "Scripturæ Linguæque Phœniciæ quotquot supersunt," par G. Gesenius, Leipsic, 1837; "Miscellanea Phœnicia," Hamaker, 1828; "Études Palæographiques sur l'histoire Phœnician," Gesenius, Leipsic, 1831; "Die Phœniziers das Phœnizische Alterthum," J. C. Movers, Berlin, 1841–6; "Missions de Phœnicie," par M. Renan in the "Histoire des langues semitiques." Renan says (p. 186) that the epigraphic monuments happily supply in part the almost complete loss of their books. Commenting upon this statement, Professor Rawlinson says, "History of Phœnicia," p. 393: "The Epigraphic literature scarcely deserves to be highly rated. It consists at present of five or six moderately long and some hundreds of exceedingly short inscriptions, the longer ones being all inscribed on stones, the shorter on stones, vases, pateræ, gems, coins, and the like." The longest of all is that on Esmunasa, King of Sidon, containing 298 words, principally occupied with directions about his sepulture and denunciations against those who may open, empty, or in any way interefere with "his chamber."

* The words most commonly in use, the particles, the pronouns, the forms of the verb, the principal inflexions (and we may add the numerals) in Phœnician are identical or nearly identical with the pure Hebrew (Renan, "Histoire des langues semitiques," pp. 189, 190). In form and

and that, having settled on the shores of the Mediterranean at the dawn of history, "Great Sidon" * eventually became their principal city. Her vessels traversed all parts of the Mediterranean, and her artificers were celebrated as the most skilful in the world.† This was one of the nations which oppressed Israel,‡ but at last the term of her empire

---

feature the Phœnicians are said to have resembled their near neighbours the Jews. The Hebrew, the Phœnician, and the Aramaic (Syro-Chaldean) seem to be derived from one language which is lost, and we are told by Theil ("Das Phœnizesche Alterthum," p. 5) that the Phœnicians were of the same race as the Canaanites. St. Augustine ("Opera Omnia," iv. 1285), speaking of the descendants of the Carthaginians in North Africa, says, "Interrogati nostri rustici—Quid Sint? Punici Respondentes Chanani." Such purely Phœnician names existed as Abimelech (Father of the King), Gen. xx. 2; Melchizedek (King of Righteousness), Gen. xiv. 18; Kirjath Separ (City of the Book), Josh. xv. 15.

* See Josh. xi. 8 and xix. 28.

† When Achilles, at the funeral of Patroclus, desired to offer as a prize to the fastest runner the most beautiful bowl that was to be found in all the world, he naturally chose one which had been deftly made by high-skilled Sidonians, and which Phœnician sailors had conveyed in one of their hollow barks across the cloud-shadowed sea (Homer, Iliad xxiii. 743, quoted by Rawlinson, "Phœnicia," p. 408).   ‡ Judg. x. 12.

ceased, and about 1252 years [*] before Christ Tyre began to reign in her stead. The latter was even declared to be a strong city in the time of Joshua, and, taking the place of its former rival, effectively commenced its work of colonisation in Spain about 1130 B.C. Caralis in Sardinia was also established,[†] and this is noteworthy in connection with the subject of Phœnician remains both there and in South-eastern Africa. Settlers were sent to Tingis and Lixus on the West African coast, as well as to Hadrumetum and the Lesser Leptis in North Africa. Sidon had plumed her wings and taken a considerable flight. Tyre rose much higher, and flew to all parts not merely of the then known world, but to the most distant and unexplored countries. It was not, however, until a comparatively recent period that Cornwall and the Scilly Islands were reached, and it was then, or within a short period after, that the city reached the culminating point of its greatness. It seems most anomalous that the details of

[*] This date is given by Kenrick in his "Phœnicia," p. 343.
[†] Claudian, "Bell. Geld.," 1–20.

the history of Phœnicia—the most advanced, civilised, and prosperous nation of antiquity—should be left without the barest outline of continuous history. But for the Scripture narrative and Josephus we should have to walk in still greater darkness. Thanks to these we know that, when King David was still in the prime of life, Hiram succeeded to the Tyrian throne, and soon became his ally and adviser. "The Sidonians and they of Tyre brought much cedar wood to David." When King Solomon succeeded his father the friendship continued, and the powerful assistance of the Tyrians was secured in building the great Temple, in the substructions of which we behold at the present day the special description of solid masonry, not joined together with mortar, so significant of the work of the Phœnicians. Then followed the erection of the King of Israel's palace,*

---

* "This palace was somewhat Assyrian in character, as it consisted of several distinct edifices. The chief was a long hall which, like the Temple, was encased in cedar, whence probably its name, 'The House of the Forest of Lebanon.' Between the palace and a portico was a cedar portico, sometimes called the 'Tower of David.' In this tower, apparently hung over the walls outside, were a

and the beauty of the throne of the House of
David was only second to that of the House
of God. Solomon and Hiram were close allies
for twenty years,* and in one respect Solomon

thousand golden shields, which gave to the whole palace
the name of Armoury. With a splendour that outshone
any like fortress, the tower with these golden targets
glittered far off in the sunshine like the tall neck, it was
thought, of a beautiful bride decked out, after the manner
of the East, with strings of golden chains. Within the
porch was to be seen the king in state. On a throne of
ivory, brought from Africa or India, the throne of many
an Arabian legend, the Kings of Judah were solemnly
seated on the day of their accession. . . . He sate on the
back of a golden bull, its head turned over its shoulder,
probably the ox or bull of Ephraim; under his feet, on
each side of the steps, were six golden lions, probably the
lions of Judah. This was the seat of judgment, this was
the throne of the House of David" (Stanley, "Lectures
on the Jewish Church," ii. 165–167, quoted by Rawlinson,
"Phœnicia," pp. 426, 427).

* It is said by Justin ("Dialogue," C. Tryph., S. 34)
that, on one occasion when King Solomon visited Tyre,
he worshipped in a Sidonian temple in order to please
his ally Hiram. Menander (*ap.* Clement Alex., "Strom.,"
i. 386) says that as a second-class wife Solomon married
one of Hiram's daughters. Certain it is that we are told
in the Scripture that "King Solomon loved many strange
women together with the daughter of Pharaoh, women
of the Moabites, Ammonites, Edomites, Sidonians, and
Hittites." In fact, the alliance of the Phœnicians became

was of immense service to the Phœnicians. He was master of the port of Ezion-Geber on the Red Sea, which indeed was established by him as a place for commerce and navigation. This harbour was the key to an enormous lucrative trade not only with Arabia and India, but also with Eastern Africa. The great trade route along the Caelo-Syrian Valley, *viâ* Aleppo and Tadmor, was also in the hands of Solomon. It will thus be seen that, by a close alliance of the Tyrian power, at its acme of greatness, with that of the Hebrew nation at its most prosperous period, great results naturally followed. Luxury fostered the love of gold and all that could gratify the desires of a sensual people. As in the case of money, so with regard to commerce, the desire of success only increases with prosperity. Now more than ever were

---

the partial destruction of the Jewish people. Eth Baal, King or High Priest of Ashtaroth, married the daughter of Jezebel to Ahab, King of Israel, and the corrupting influence thus introduced caused the destruction of the Israelitish kingdom. Jezebel's daughter Athaliah became the wife of Ahaziah, King of Judah, and the prophet Ezekiel tells us that the heathen rites then introduced were among the chief causes of the Captivity.

immense efforts made by the most skilful mariners, miners, and colonists of antiquity. Arabia was treated as the pivot or point of departure, and Ophirs of the southern seas were opened to the world. It is probably to a period shortly before the establishment of large Tyrian commercial relations with Ezion-Geber that we may trace the first visit of Phœnician Nature worshippers to Monomotapa, where they built the colossal edifices whose remains now stand sphynx-like for explanation.

We shall see in the sequel that the aboriginal or early people of South-eastern Africa were comparatively mild, intelligent, and docile. It was not until late in the fifteenth or early in the sixteenth century that the fierce Zulus rushed on the Mashonas of Monomotapa as the Huns and Goths hurled themselves on European civilisation. Consequently Phœnician or Arabian colonists could have found no great difficulty in forming a settlement. We shall try to show that the people who did come extracted much gold from the mines, and that they probably settled in the country, and by means of marriage amalgamated with its people.

The subject of the Colonies of Phœnicia is of great consequence. This great seafaring people evidently perceived that for mining and mercantile purposes colonies were essential. As Britain acted eighteen hundred years after Christ, so did Phœnicia more than one thousand years before the birth of our Saviour. Cyprus, Cilicia, and Memphis in Egypt were among the first places colonised, and Herodotus tells us (i. 1) that the Phœnicians dealt largely in the wares of Egypt. There is little doubt that Tarsus (Cilicia) was at first a Phœnician colony, then came Syria and Amathus and Paphos, Rhodes and the islands of the Ægean Sea, North Africa from the Lesser Syrtis to Hippo-Regius. They then rested for three centuries, and towards the middle of the ninth century B.C. romantic legends inform us of an aristocratic exodus from Tyre which resulted in the foundation of Carthage, which eventually became so powerful as to fight with Rome for the supremacy of the world. The remains of this once celebrated mart of nations are now scarcely discernible, but recent explorers have, by means of excavations, uncovered cyclopean walls thoroughly Phœnician in character, and belonging probably to the most* early period. This greatest of the colonies of its parent country itself sent out colonies, and the famous Periplus of Hanno commences with the words, "It was decreed by the Carthaginians that Hanno should undertake a voyage beyond the Pillars of Hercules, and there found Liby-Phœnician cities. Phœnician races, certainly people who practised the Phœnician religion, peopled settlements in Sardinia, and mines were worked there whose produce was no doubt exchanged for articles of commerce brought from Carthage and Tyre. Spain became one of the greatest and richest

---

* "On Carthage and her Remains." See the work of this title by Dr. N. Davis, F.R.G.S., &c. London, Richard Bentley, 1861. This writer describes the ruins. He says (p. 279), "However great the idolatry of the Phœnicians may have been, and however degraded the practices connected with the worship of their deities, one idea appears to have invaded their minds, and that is, that it was impossible for man to make any adequate and comprehensive representation of the Godhead." In fact, in early times stone worship—conic stones, pillars, and towers—were the objects of worship. This was the case in Carthage, Tyre, Arabia, and Abyssinia, as well as in Monomotapa at our Zimbabwes.

of the Phœnician colonies,* and the Casseterides was a flourishing settlement where immense supplies of tin, lead, and copper extracted from the mines of Cornwall, the Scilly Isles, &c., and Leinster, in Ireland, were exchanged for pottery, salt, and vessels of bronze. But the people who circumnavigated Africa and dared the fierce waters of the North Atlantic were not likely to cramp their exertions in the waters of the Southern hemisphere. A port was obtained from King Solomon on the Red Sea, an intimate religious maritime and commercial alliance existed with Arabia, and we cannot doubt that this adventurous people made the most of these advantages. The Arabs, however, were so intimately connected with the colonisation and settlements of the Southern Ocean that we must consider all history there in connection with that of this great ancient people. They held exactly the stone worship of the early Sidonian and Tyrian periods, and their monuments and

* Strabo tells us that in a very early age, shortly after the Trojan war, the Phœnicians founded the colonies of Gades (Cadiz), of Malaga, Abdera, and Carteia. See on this subject and that of Phœnician Colonies Kenrick's "Phœnicia," pp. 118–122.

inscriptions prove that they unquestionably practised the same religion as that professed by the men who built the South African Zimbabwes.

Phœnicia was prosperous for a thousand years. It was the carrying, colonising, and commercial power of that time. The riches of all parts of the known world, and many parts of the comparatively unknown world, flowed to its ports, were conveyed in its ships, and built up a corrupting system of luxury where impurity and cruelty struggled for mastery. Phœnicia passed through many vicissitudes. She became the tributary of Assyria, and then recovered freedom only to lose it again in a contest with Babylon. Still in the midst of disasters she kept the dominion of the sea, and it was when Egypt was struggling against the Babylonian power that the King (Neco) of the former country received aid from the Phœnicians in the construction of those fleets which, placed on the Mediterranean and Red Sea, were sent out in the Phœnician expedition to which we have already referred, which circumnavigated Africa. In 585 B.C. Nebuchadnezzar reduced

Tyre, and sixty years afterwards submitted to Cambyses, and refused to obey his order when he commanded its people to make war on Carthage. Persian rule was succeeded by an alliance with Egypt, and then came the scourge of God—Alexander the Great. The great emporium of nations defied him and utterly perished. In 332 Tyre ceased to be a city, and although for a short time its commerce and importance were revived, it was not long before the prophecies of Scripture were literally verified. In the words of Ezekiel—

"And they shall weep for thee in bitterness of soul with
    bitter mourning,
And in their wailing they shall take up a lamentation
    for thee,
And lament over thee saying, Who is there like Tyre,
Like her that is brought to silence in the midst of the
    sea?
When thy wares went forth out of the seas thou filledst
    many people,
Thou didst enrich the kings of the earth with thy mer-
    chandise and thy riches.
In the time that thou wast broken by the seas in the
    depth of the waters,
Thy merchandise and all thy company didst fall in the
    midst of thee,
All the inhabitants of the isles are astonished at thee,

And their kings are sore afraid, they are troubled in their countenance.

The merchants that are among the peoples hiss at thee;

Thou art become a terror and thou shall never be any more."

BOOK II.

ARABIA.

So far as it is possible to judge, it seems probable that it was people of Saba, in Arabia Felix, who in their own, or in Phœnician ships, landed on the coast of Sofala, penetrated to the mines, and established a colony there. With reference to this subject a general review of Arabian history seems desirable. Arabia is regarded by very great and competent authorities as the primitive centre of the formation of the Semitic races, and we are told that " the study of the actual populations of Eastern Africa proves that from an epoch which is lost in the night of time the relations between Arabia and Africa were very important and very numerous." *

* V. Maury, " La Terre et l'Homme," p. 408. The country of the Arabs and the Somalis (in Abyssinia) are styled in a general way the country of " Punt " in a document of the fifteenth century B.C. See Masperi, p. 169.

Their geographical propinquity renders this easy to believe, and we know that monuments expressive of the Phœnician religion are to be found, not only in Monomotapa (sometimes styled Lower Ethiopia), but also in the famous kingdom of Prester John, or Upper Ethiopia.*

* In "The Sacred City of the Ethiopians," by J. Theodore Bent, F.S.A., F.R.G.S., London, Longmans, Green & Co., 1893, we are told (p. 83), "Here in Abyssinia Christianity must have succeeded a form of Sabæan Sun worship; the monoliths and altars all point to this." "The greater part of the wall of the temple at Yeha is of late construction, and let into it are two fragments with Himyaritic inscriptions upon them. In front of the vestibule stood two rough monoliths, at the base of one of which is an altar with a circular disc. . . . The priests had two Sabæan inscriptions hidden away in this church" (p. 140). "The ruined fortress must be Ava, destroyed possibly in the days of the Ptolemies, and the capital of Ethiopia Trogloditica before the town of Aksum was built. Many points beside the name seemed to confirm this theory—the obvious antiquity of the building, the rude monoliths, and the Himyaritic inscriptions—and then absolute confirmation arrived from Professor D. H. Muller, who, in one of the inscriptions found at Yeha, read the words, ' His house or temple Awa.' Hence we have Ava as the principal city of a Sabæan civilisation, with a temple and monoliths and Sun worship, conquered by an overwhelming army which spread over Ethiopia, the victories of which are recorded on the Adulitan stone" (p. 145). Ludolphus, in his history written in 1684, says

ARABIA.

People of Arabian race may have settled in both separately, or possibly migrated to the south from the north in pursuit of those treasures about which rumours, reports, and traditions existed.

Here, however, are two great countries, Arabia and Abyssinia, in which unquestionably in very early periods existed Nature worship of the Phœnicians, expressed in that

of the Ethiopians, "For they are not natives of the land, but came out of that part of Arabia which is called 'The Happy,' which adjoins the Red Sea" (p. 175). "That an Arabian colony settled on this coast at a very remote time is absolutely proved by the mass of Himyaritic inscriptions found there. . . . That this Arabian colony, cut off from its mother country, gradually lost its identity, merging with the negroid races around them, may be taken for granted from the blended physique which is characteristic even of the Ethiopian of the day" (p. 175). "In vain we look for information" (about ancient Abyssinia) "in the pages of Edrese, Aboulfeda, and Ibn Said; their knowledge was very meagre and their pictures of the country ridiculous. As Gibbon says, 'Encompassed by the enemies of their religion, the Ethiopians slept for a thousand years, forgetful of the world, by whom they were forgotten'" (p. 179). "The first object to be seen on approaching Aksum is a tall monolith, twenty feet in height, hewn out of granite . . . and there are several others prostrate near it" (p. 180). "The great rows of obelisks up the valley call, however, for our peculiar litholatry so strangely spread over the world. The sermons in stone which comprise a revelation of the religion of the Himyaritic people of South Arabia are very numerous, and have been so faithfully copied by the photographic art as to enable us to study them with ease.*

special attention, the others being merely rough, unhewn stones, like the menhirs of Brittany, the monoliths of Zimbabwe in Mashonaland, and the Stonehenge of Wiltshire" (p. 182). "The Aksumites then adapted the fashion in art to their special form of cult, namely, a veneration for stones set up in honour of the celestial deity" (p. 190). "The small Sabæan inscriptions found by Mr. Bent in Yeha, the old temple near Adoua, unfortunately do not provide us with the name of any king or any date. . . . They testify by their presence there to the connection between the peoples of South Arabia and of Abyssinia which is set forth in the lists of peoples in the tenth chapter of Genesis; and they also testify to the migration into Ethiopia of the Sabæans—a fact which Greek authors allude to. That these were not isolated or sporadic colonisations is testified by the magnificence of the buildings themselves. . . . We are also in the position, from palæographic grounds, to assert that these small fragments, as well as the buildings into which they were built, date from a very remote antiquity, about the seventh or eighth century B.C." (p. 232).

* A magnificent series of photographs of votive stones, &c., from Arabia will be found in the "Corpus Inscriptionum Semiticarum ab Academia Inscriptionum et

The first dawning gleams which can be obtained of history point to the fact that Arabia was under the domination of the Kahtanee Arabs, who were of southern origin. As in Ireland, so in Arabia: there were numerous kings, and their aristocratic monarchical systems are described as forming a framework round the central wilds of the peninsula. Yemen was the oldest and greatest of these kingdoms, and we know that their monarchs were styled descendants of Kahtan Hamyar (the dusky). The latter of these names is distinctly African, and when we find that to this was added the surname "Tobba," which is a word of African etymology meaning powerful, there is little doubt of their intimate connection with the neigh-

Literum humaniorum conditum atque digestum. Pars Prima-Inscriptiones Phœnicias continens," Paris, 1881. Mr. Edward Glaser, in his works on Yemen published under the auspices of the Academy of Inscriptions, refers to great ruins made of huge rough stones which he found on a hill. In Arabia materials have been taken away much more than in South-east Africa. Palgrave in his travels refers to megalithic vestiges of enormous stones, comprising large boulders, each fourteen feet high, placed on end, and originally crowned by a similar horizontal series.

bouring continent. For 2,500 years the Kings of Yemen held sway over the destinies of a brave and enterprising people, but their deeds, adventures, and glories are as if they had been written in sand. The glory of the world has long passed away from a race of rulers who are said to have subdued Central Asia and even reached the confines of China on the path which they had made as conquerors.

The first great fact in the history of Arabia with which we have to deal is the conquest of Edom by King Solomon and his establishment of the port of Ezion-Geber at the head of the Elamitic Gulf not far from Elath. Here was a new port opened to the Phœnicians one thousand years before Christ. The sacred Scriptures tell us that King Solomon caused a fleet to be constructed at Ezion-Geber, "which is near Elath on the shores of the Red Sea, in the country of Edom; and Hiram, King of Tyre, sent his servants, seamen, and men who understood the sea, and they brought four hundred and twenty talents of gold to King Solomon." Now where did this immense amount of gold come from? We are answered in the Bible that "Ophir" was the source of supply, and it is therefore of consequence to discover where this auriferous country was situated. The subject has been one of keen controversy, but we think, if it be fairly and dispassionately considered, there can be no hesitation in arriving at the conclusion that at least one of the Ophirs of Scripture—for there may have been another on the Malabar coast of India—was situated inland from the Sofala coast in the realm of Monomotapa. It was because of this gold that people who practised the same religion as that of Phœnicia built our Zimbabwes, and only the quest of treasure and the desire to retain it when acquired could have prompted the erection of such buildings. One of the greatest and keenest critics * who has given this subject

---

* M. Quatremere, in his work published in 1846. We follow his arguments. See him very fully quoted by M. Guillain in his "Documents sur l'Histoire, la Géographie, et le Commerce de l'Afrique Orientale, publié par ordre du Gouvrement," Première Partie, p. 10. M. Guillain heartily concurs with M. Quatremere's views, and is confident that the Ophir of Scripture was at Sofala on the South-east coast of Africa. Gosselin, in

his attention considers that ancient Ophir must have been situated on the South-eastern Coast of Africa (Sofala Monomotapa), or on the Malabar coast of India, or in Arabia Felix. The last supposition can be very easily put aside, as the distance from Ezion-Geber to any other port of Arabia is too short to require the three years of navigation which we know had to be undertaken to go to Ophir and return; besides, Arabia was not a gold-producing country, neither was it a land of elephants from which ivory could be procured. One argument which has been used is that in the minds of the Jews the Queen of Sheba who visited Solomon was inseparably connected with the land of Ophir. No doubt in commerce her country was intimately connected with Ophir, but of course it does

---

his "Récherches sur la géographique systematique et positive des Anciens," tome xi., p. 91, is strangely of opinion that Ophir was in Arabia Felix, so is Michaelis in his "Spicilegium Geographiæ exteræ," tome ii., p. 84, but D'Anville is decidedly of opinion that Ophir was in South-east Africa (see "Mémoire sur le pays d'Ophir ou les flottes de Salomon allaient chercher l'or," par M. D'Anville, in "Mémoires de litérature tirès des registres de l'Academie Royale," &c., pp. 83–93).

not necessarily follow that the place was in Arabia.

The arguments for the Malabar coast are much more powerful, but they are quite inadequate to prove that it was the only "Ophir." Two of the arguments in favour of this opinion are founded on the facts that *algummin*, or sandalwood, and *toukkun*, or peacocks, must have been obtained there. We are told that if the ships of the Jews and Tyrians had sailed to Malabar or any port in India, the merchandise which would have been carried to such places—silk, cotton, perfumes, and pepper—would have been stated. Then there is the statement that India has never furnished large quantities of gold to the commercial world. In fact, it was frequently an article of import into that country. So far as ivory is concerned, it is well known that Asiatic elephants were from time immemorial made use of as beasts of burden, and that their value in this way prevented their slaughter. In Africa, on the other hand, they have been always hunted and never domesticated. Of course too much stress cannot be laid upon words which do not specially mean "peacocks" or "sandal-wood," but are generic terms for birds of fine plumage and scented wood. The former may have been paraquets, and Africa produces numerous trees which could come under the category symbolised by the term "sandal."

When we come to consider the claims of Monomotapa to be the Ophir of Scriptures, we find numerous important authorities, including Bruce, D'Anville, Quatremere, and Guillain, in our favour. In the first place, there is no doubt that gold was the principal export of Ophir, and the workings of the ancient mines, Arab tradition, and Portuguese history all concur in showing that the mines of Monomotapa were exceedingly rich, and that an immense quantity of valuable ore was extracted from them. Quatremere says: "What part of the globe, before the discovery of the new continent, has produced throughout all ages the greatest quantity of gold? All the world replies that it is Africa; and even to-day it seems that this part of the earth is able to produce gold in greater quantity than even America itself. . . . In the Middle Ages the Arabs, not less commercial and not less avaricious than the Phœnicians, made frequent voyages to the East Coast of Africa and into the island of Madagascar, from whence, above all things, they brought gold. . . . A passage in the Book of Job seems to bear out my opinion when he mentions 'gold dust.' This expression, which is translated very exactly by the words 'glebæ aŭri,' designates, I believe, gold in powder such as is received with so much abundance from the sands of Africa."

As to ivory, it is scarcely necessary to dwell upon the notorious fact that during all ages an immense quantity has been obtained from Africa. The elephants in that part of the world have always been merely game, not assistants to man in the occupations of life, and their slaughter has been the persistent occupation of hunters for two thousand years.

Huet, who is the author of an able treatise on the voyages of Solomon published at the commencement of the eighteenth century, declares that he feels compelled to accept the fact that the place styled Ophir from which gold was fetched by the combined Jewish and Tyrian fleet was unquestionably on the Southeast Coast of Africa, in that part known under the names of Mozambique and Sofala; that at the time when King Solomon reigned the Hebrew and Phœnician navigators traded with these shores, and that this commerce was anterior to the exact period referred to in Scripture. For the gold of Ophir was known to the Idumeans before the time of David, and the Book of Paralipomenon (The Chronicles) records the fact that this prince reserved a portion of it. "To seek out the origin of this commercial movement we must go back to those hardy pioneers who were able to show the Phœnicians the geographical position of Ophir and lead them to the mines of gold." This is indeed true. The fleet of King Solomon and Hiram never discovered Ophir, although it is probable that they placed miners and merchants as settlers there. Its treasures were known previously, and we are therefore now confronted with the fact that some of the Zimbabwes of Monomotapa were built more than one thousand years before the Christian era. That a settlement did exist there can scarcely be a doubt, and that a colony obtaining much gold would feel the necessity of forts and therefore build them is a reasonable conclusion. They built as the Phœnicians built at Sidon, in Tyre, in Sardinia, and in Carthage. Their religion was litholatry, and they erected edifices exactly similar to those raised by their Himyaritic brethren in Arabia. For these epochs our books of history are epigraphic. It is by means of sermons in stones that we learn the religion, the architecture, and therefore the origin of those people whose monuments form the Sphynxes of Southern Africa.

The peninsula of Arabia is admirably situated for purposes of commerce. The Red Sea stretches upwards along its western coast to give it an opportunity of uniting the trade of the northern and the southern hemispheres. On the other side the Persian Gulf forms a great waterway for Oriental commerce. No impartial writer can fail to see that the near coast of Malabar was visited. Indeed, Phœnician monuments prove the fact, and the rich produce of the East no doubt entitled this land, including probably Ceylon, and perhaps Sumatra, to be enrolled in the category of "Ophirs."

Nevertheless the preponderance of evidence is decidedly in favour of the principal Ophir of Scripture having been inland from the Sofala coast, in the country of Monomotapa.

Arabia, like Africa, is somewhat a barren nurse, and the comparatively small portion of the country which is fertile compelled the inhabitants from the most remote ages to turn their attention to the navigation of the sea and commerce. As the Phœnicians were the carriers of the northern world, so were the Arabs the marine purveyors of the southern ocean. If there be any feature more striking or remarkable than another in Arabian history it is the extreme secretiveness of the nation. Ten centuries after the vessels of the Tyrians and Syrians had ploughed southern seas we are told of the wonderful discovery of monsoons in the Indian Ocean by Hippalus. Of course they were known to the Arabians during all that period, and naturally they used the knowledge, and benefited by it. Then what extreme reticence must they have preserved as to the situations and character of the places with which they traded. We have seen already that, according to Strabo, the master of a Phœnician bark preferred to lose his vessel on the rocks of the Cassiterides rather than permit a Roman ship which followed to gain a knowledge of a safe channel to a valuable port. The secret of gold was kept quite as carefully as any other and for even more powerful reasons.

As far as authentic history reaches we have a knowledge of the fact that cassia and cinnamon were imported into Egypt from Tyre. In the sacred writings Moses speaks of myrrh, cassia, and cinnamon. Nineveh, Babylon, and Thebes required and received the wealth obtained by the traders of the Indian Ocean. The Hindoos were never a maritime people, and their religion forbade them to pass the Indus, while political and religious prejudices affected the Persians and the Egyptians. One of the most competent authorities,* after reviewing the entire

* M. Guillain. "Documents sur l'Histoire, la Geographie, et le Commerce de l'Afrique Orientale, publié par ordre du Gouvrement," Paris, Bertrand, Première Partie, p. 39.

evidence with respect to the situation of Ophir, and positively deciding in favour of its having been situated in South-east Africa, concludes by saying: "From all the reasons derived from analogy and history which we have considered, we believe it to be sufficiently proved that Arabia has been from time immemorial the centre of commerce between the people of the East and the coast populations of the Mediterranean; that the Arabs delivered the products of these countries to the commerce of the Phœnicians and Egyptians; that the Arabs in time immemorial discovered the part of Africa situated to the south-east, and frequented it as far down at least as Sofala; finally, that other people did not arrive there until after them, and by means of them. . . . All the people who have visited the eastern shores of Africa—Hebrews, Tyrians, Egyptians, Greeks, Romans, and even the Portuguese, have only passed along. . . . The establishment and domination of the Arabs have preceded and survived them." What a wonderful retrospective vista is opened to us!

It has been well said of Arab literature that it is specially rich in works of imagination, but that the books which have come down to us in the shape of histories are more pictorial and poetical than correct. Myths, mythic tales, and mythological fables abound, but the substance of reality is wanting. There are many poets, and under the Arab Caliphs of Damascus science even was wonderfully advanced; but, after all, the greatest literary monument of this nation which has come down to our time is the celebrated "Thousand and One Nights," probably composed in Bagdad in the twelfth century. Sinbad had evidently been a traveller along the weird and wonderful shores of South-eastern Africa. Several voyagers refer to the mountains of Adamant on the Abyssinian coast, and it was difficult even for him to exaggerate the wealth of Ophir, while the mines of diamonds seem to have existed in prophecy as well as in imagination.

We have already referred to the circumnavigation of Africa by Phœnicians six hundred years before Christ, under the orders of Necho, King of Egypt. About one hundred years before the Christian era Eudoxus is said to have visited and found most extraordinary human beings, who were only able to make themselves understood by means of signs, as some of them had no tongues and others who had were not able to use them. They also possessed, instead of mouths, small holes in which, when hungry, they could only introduce one grain of corn at a time. Fire was so unknown that when seen by them for the first time it was embraced with transports, and they only ceased to hug it when compelled by pain to desist. The first of these extraordinary narratives is found in Pomponius Mela, and it only forms an extract from a lost work of Cornelius Nepos, who, in his turn, took it from an unknown source. Intrinsically it is a romance, but even extrinsically it has been proved to be one of two contradictory stories. Africa has been the portion of the globe from which something new was always expected, and always obtained. The most extraordinary races of mankind existed amidst its vast deserts, mountains, and plains. No fiction was too wonderful, and nothing seemed too surprising or absurd for belief.*

* The old English books are full of fictions and romances about Africa, extracted generally from conti-

The ancient Greeks and Romans entertained the most extraordinary and incorrect ideas about Africa. Homer, nine hundred years before Christ, conducts Neptune into Ethiopia, and places the inhabitants of this country in his category of naked people. Herodotus, four hundred years later, writes of the Phœnician circumnavigation of Africa, and then comes the Periplus of Scylax of Cariander who, under the orders of King Darius, descended the Indus to the sea and coasted along Arabia. It seems, however,

nental sources. The British Museum Library retains carefully, as a scarce book, a work translated from the French and published in the time of Queen Elizabeth, which narrates all the tales of Eudoxus as if they were perfectly correct. We are told that the Africans "Be very lowe men but marveylous blacke," and that they never live longer than forty years, as before the end of that period they are eaten up by fleas. On the title-page the reader is called upon "To mark inwardly" and pay great attention to the instructive text. "Purchas his Pilgrimage" narrates with great gravity many extraordinary things, and so indeed do all the books of the period. Purchas seems only to draw the line at the statement of the existence of Amazons. This is too much for his credibility, but other much more unlikely statements are recorded without hesitation or the semblance of a doubt.

that the Persians were averse to navigation and had no ships of their own in the Indian Ocean, or even in the Persian Gulf — Phœnicians being their principal mariners. Ctesias, a physician at the Court of Persia, under Artaxerxes Mnemon, wrote a number of absurd fables about India, but when we come to the time of Alexander the Great, seventy years later, we find the great Aristotle affirming that the earth was round and showing a knowledge of most remote islands in the southern hemisphere. Malte Brun, the French geographer, says: "The modern critic is astonished to find Aristotle naming Taprobane long before the age of the Ptolemies, and even indicating the isle of Madagascar, named *Phanbalon* by the Arabs." When the northern world was subdued by Alexander he sent Nearchus to descend the river Indus, and to return by the Persian Gulf and the Euphrates. No doubt great results followed, and we know that soon after the establishment of Alexandria it became the centre of commerce between Asia, Arabia, South-eastern Africa, and the littoral of the Mediterranean. Subsequently the ships of

Egypt penetrated into the Red Sea, and traded with the nations to the south. Alexandria became not merely the headquarters of commerce but of literature. Geography and history were specially represented, but the books written on these subjects were destroyed. Names survive, such as those of Eratosthenes, Agatharchides, Artemidorus, and Hipparchus, but only fractions of their writings have come down to us in the works of other authors. Strabo, Pliny, and Diodorus, quoting the Alexandrian writers, tell us that the commerce of Egypt extended down the Red Sea. No doubt they traded with the Sabæan Arabs of Yemen, who kept to themselves the knowledge of the gold mines of South Africa. The keeper of the great Alexandrian library (Eratosthenes) tells us that the country of the Sabæans abounds in perfumes to such a remarkable extent that the natives are obliged to attenuate the force of them by odours of an opposite description. The men are robust* warriors, and skilful mariners. They embark in great vessels, and

---

* The Prophet Isaiah refers to the people of Sabæa as of high stature.

sail towards the countries which produce odoriferous substances; they establish colonies there." He informs us that there does not exist on the earth any nation as rich as the Sabæans and people of Gerha (a seaport town of Arabia). They possessed a profusion of objects of luxury, and in their manner of living equal the magnificence of princes. This country is so fortunately situated as to retain its independence in consequence of its distance from Europe; but for this circumstance the Sabæans would soon have been reduced to the condition of agents, whereas northern nations were actually obliged to accept them as the masters of commerce. Certainly this proves that in the second and first centuries before Christ the Greek rulers of Egypt had to make Saba a terminal point, and use it as an *entrepôt*. In the days of the Ptolemies the Arabians enjoyed a great monopoly and what was called the "Indian trade," by means of which large numbers of slaves were constantly brought from Africa.

The conquest of Egypt by Augustus (B.C. 30) seems to have effected no alteration in the course of Red Sea trade, but the expedition of Aelius Gallus sent against Arabia points to the fact that the monopoly of the Sabæans had become galling. It was not until forty-seven years after Christ that Hippalus discovered the monsoons for northern mariners, and these were soon taken advantage of.

The Periplus of the Erythræan Sea, attributed to Arrien, an Egyptian Greek, is supposed to have been written in the reign of Septimus Severus about the year 210, and we learn from it that after passing the country of Azania, the ocean which "has not been navigated" turns towards the setting sun, and taking on the reverse the coasts of Ethiopia, of Libya, and of Africa, joins the western sea. "These places are almost the last." The Periplus, in describing the ports of South-east Africa, tells us that Tabia supplies various descriptions of perfumes and incense, while Opone furnishes besides a large number of very good slaves. Rhapta is governed by a king who has under his control people who attend to ships. We are brought to the place subsequently known as Mombasa, and to the island of Zanzibar, perhaps to Mozambique, but the difficulty of fixing where the places are is very considerable. Mariners of Tyre and Ptolemy give us no satisfactory information, and indeed intense ignorance prevailed in Europe regarding the geography of the southern hemisphere until a comparatively recent date. A piece of information of some consequence gained from the Periplus regards the system of rule in colonies and settlements on the South-east Coast of Africa. It seems that the plan of having a chief in each was prevalent, and in accordance with Arabian customs there would probably have been little governmental interference from Arabia. So long as the mines were worked and trade prospered the Home Government was probably content. Certainly, so far as the great southern seas were concerned, Phœnicia ceased to be a factor of any consequence after the conquest of Tyre by Alexander the Great. Arabs were everywhere over the great southern seas, trading with their own colonies and settlements as well as with other countries, conducting navigation and ruling commerce.

With the native population of Monomotapa no doubt the mining settlers mingled and intermarried. As they acted in other parts of Africa so did they act in the land of Ophir. There was, no doubt, from the very earliest times a large admixture of the blood, religion, and customs of Arabia in all Ethiopia—Upper and Lower. We have no records of events in the very early ages to which we are adverting. To Europe the land was a *terra incognita*, and the fact has to be received that for more than two thousand years a partially civilised people mined and traded with Arabia, whose only records are the ruins of towers and temples scattered throughout a land whose inhabitants were eventually subjugated by the most cruel barbarians who have ever disgraced the name of man in Africa. These last in turn gave place to the people of a country which is the Phœnicia of the modern world.

Before the time of Mahomet a knowledge of South-east Africa scarcely can be said to have existed in Europe. Cosmas, one of the famous Christian geographers, mixes up

Barbary and Ethiopia inextricably, and tells us that the Queen of Saba was queen of the south and offered King Solomon spices which she had obtained from Barbary, "which is a place separated from her States by a gulf." He also refers to treasures and to monkeys, as well as to the gold of Ethiopia, which he declares to be a place situated on the confines of the earth. Christian Abyssinians conquered the Himyarites of Arabia, and the latter in the year 601 called upon Chosroes II., King of Persia, to come to their aid; and shortly afterwards near Aden the Ethiopian king was slain, after his nation had ruled in Saba for seventy-two years. It does not seem that under any circumstances commercial activity slackened, but in truth the great spirit of independence and love of Ishmaelitic freedom never made it possible for Arabia to consolidate her rule and build up an empire. Indeed there never appears to have been any desire for consolidation.

For a long time there was an alliance between Constantinople and Arabia. The Emperor Justinian sent ambassadors to Yemen, and one of his principal objects was to prevent the Persians having a monopoly of the valuable silk trade. However, under Chosroes the Great we find Persia succeeding in obtaining the lion's share of Arabian commerce. Indeed alternate nations in accordance with their power and influence used the ports of Yemen as *entrepôts*. The first on record were the Tyrians and Hebrews, to be followed by the Greeks of Alexandria, and subsequently by the Romans, Byzantines, and Persians. We are informed that up to this time the Arabs were neither colonisers nor conquerors. Guillain says that in many of the ports with which they traded transactions were effectually carried on without risk and in perfect liberty without the intervention of any Arab authority. Briefly, enterprising travellers and adroit traders, the Arabs had not been up to this time either colonisers or conquerors. Nevertheless gold was continually produced from the rich mines of Monomotapa by the mixed race, partly Phœnician, partly Arabian, but probably chiefly of African origin.

The appearance of Mahomet and the nature of his religion, together with the circumstances attending its first wonderful successes, changed altogether the attitude of Arabia to South-east Africa, and an endeavour must be made to go down the stream of time in company with some of the principal writers from whose pages any information can be procured. It must be borne in mind that within a century and a half from the death of Mahomet, Islamism covered Africa. A chronicle which the Portuguese discovered at Quiloa, when that place was taken, gives us the information that in the year 129 of the Hegira (739 of Christ) a number of defeated insurgents, styled the Emozeides, left Arabia and settled in Africa. This was only the beginning of an expansion continued at frequent intervals. The most intimate relations also existed between the two countries, as we find that the people of Zendj, which had now become the Arabian name for an immense portion of the south-eastern continent of Africa, furnished a large portion of the army of the Caliphs of Bagdad, while subsequently the southern part of Mesopotamia was invaded by bands of warriors from the same country.*

* "Chronicle of Aboulfeda," vol. ii. p. 228.

It is interesting to notice the manner in which Africa is described by the principal Arabian writers. Massoude [*] tells us that the Nile advances through that part of the country of the Soudan which borders on Zendj, and one branch is detached and flows into the sea of Zendj. This may probably be the Zambesi. This author then goes on to describe the island of Cambalou, off the African coast, which has for inhabitants Mussulmen who speak the language of Zendj. The inhabitants were conquered at the end of the dynasty of the Ommiades and when that of the Abassides was about to commence. "Navigators advance over the sea of Zendj as far as the island of Cambalou and Sofala (low country), of Dem-

[*] Ma'Coudy Abu l Hacan-Ali was born at Bagdad about the year 890 and died in 947. Among his works are "The Meadows of Gold and Mines of Precious Stones." The first volume of this book comprises the history of the world from the Creation to the time of Mahomet; the second from the time of the False Prophet to the age in which the author wrote. De Guignes has furnished a complete analysis of this work in his "Extraits et Notices des Manuscrits." There is also a translation by Barbier de Maynard and Pavet de Courteille published in 1861.

dema, which is at the extremity of the country of Zendj. The merchants of Syraf are in the habit of navigating this sea. I have myself made a voyage, sailing from Sohhar which is the capital on Oman, with the Sarafiens who are the proprietors of the vessels. . . . The inhabitants of the people of Zendj extend to Sofala, which is the termination of the voyages of the mariners of Oman and Syraf. . . . It is a land abounding in gold, rich in wonderful things, and very fertile. The Zendjs have chosen it for the seat of their empire and have placed at their head a king, whom they name *Ouklimen*—that is the name which the King of Zendj has borne throughout all time. Eklimn, who is the chief of all the Zendj kings, marches at the head of three hundred thousand cavaliers; they are all mounted upon cows; they have neither horses nor mules, and they do not know these animals. They are not acquainted with either snow or hail. There are races among them who have pointed teeth and who eat each other. . . . The title of the King of Zendj is *Ouklimen*, which means the son of the great Master, the

God of Heaven and of earth. They call the Creator Tamkalandjalou. . . . Elephants are extremely common in the country of Zendj, but all are wild, and they do not tame any, neither do they serve in war, but are merely sought for the purpose of being killed. Oxen are used by them in combats, which bear saddles and bridles and run almost with the swiftness of horses. . . . According to the Zendjs their kings have been chosen by God to govern them and to treat them with justice. So soon as a king departs from the principles of justice he may be put to death, for they assert when the monarch conducts himself badly he ceases to be the son of the Lord of Heaven and earth. The Zendjs are very eloquent and have orators who harangue the people in their language."

De Barros,* the Portuguese writer, reproduces from Arab chronicles information respecting the foundation of several towns and the character of their inhabitants. From this source we learn that a great number of Arabs emigrated in three ships

* "First Decade of Asia," by De Barros, book viii., chapter iv.

under the command of seven brothers who fled from the persecutions of the Sultan of Bahharin. The first city they founded in Africa was Magadaxo (Moguedchou), afterwards that of Braoua, which was still, on the arrival of the Portuguese, ruled in the manner of a republic by twelve chiefs who were the descendants of the seven brothers just alluded to. Moguedchou became a powerful state, and imposed its rule over the Arabs of the coast. Among the first who came into this country were the Emoziades, who quarrelled about religious matters, and retiring into the interior mingled with the Kaffirs and adopted their customs. They subsequently formed a mixed population intermediate between the Arabs and the Kaffirs. "It was the people of Magadaxo who with their ships first reached the country of Sofala, and commercially exploited the gold mines of that region." According to the chronicle of Quiloa, a little more than seventy years after the foundation of Moguedchou and of Braoua, about the year 1000 after Christ, there reigned at Schiraz, a town of the Persian Gulf, a Moorish king, Sultan Hhacen, who left seven sons. One of these, named Ali, was looked down upon because he was the son of an Abyssinian slave, and eventually, with his family and a number of friends, left Arabia in two ships for the African coast so much celebrated for its mines of gold. He successfully arrived at Moguedchou and at Braoua, in both of which places the people were Mahometans, whereas he himself believed in the Persian religion, and therefore could not agree with them. At last he fixed his habitation at Quiloa, where he founded a state and built a fort to defend himself against the attacks of both Kaffirs and Moors. We are given a list of the successors of Ali, and when we come to the twelfth, named Daoud, are informed that in his reign one of his subjects reached Sofala and found there a vessel of Moguedchou trading in gold. One of the conditions which the people of the auriferous regions (Monomotapa) imposed upon the commercial men who trafficked with them was that each year some of their young men should be brought to become husbands to their daughters because the " Kaffirs looked upon them as a superior race." Quiloa made a similar treaty when it became a participator in the gold trade. Subsequently, when relations became developed, the Sultan of Quiloa founded an establishment at Monomotapa, whose Governors were appointed by him; this ended in a monopoly of the gold traffic being secured. Sofala and the entire country of Monomotapa seems to have been ruled from Quiloa during a long succession of years by the descendants of Daoud, until at last Pedro Alvarez Capral, Joan de Nova, and at last Vasco da Gama compelled these monarchs to declare themselves tributaries to the kings of Portugal.

So far as can be ascertained, Moguedchou was founded about 930 years after Christ, and there seems but small doubt that the political establishment of Arabs at Sofala can be shown to have taken place about 1100. We cannot say that there ever existed between Arabia and Monomotapa any colonial tie— indeed there could not be said to have been any Arabian colonies on the South-eastern Coast of Africa. All Zendj was a strange country with which certainly they traded, and to which at various times settlements went forth; but when the emigrants had founded a town they ruled it without any reference to the country of their origin. It is impossible to write the history of any of these settlements or of the great country on which they were a fringe. The Arab accounts are few, full of evident errors, and more occupied sometimes with efforts of imagination* than with a sober record of facts.

Abou-Zeid-Hassan,† who lived in the tenth century, furnishes a description of the land of Zendj, where there are several kings waging war with each other who employ as soldiers men held by chains fastened to rings passed

---

* The chroniclers say, "The navigators of Oman who frequent the sea of Zendj are Arabs of the tribe of Azd, and when traversing it, seeing their vessels sometimes elevated high and then plunged into abysses of water, they cry out—

"'O, Beurberi and Jofanni and thy enchanted billows! Jafanni and Beurberi and their billows are as thou seest.'

On the coasts of the sea of Zendj there are mountains of Adamant which cause ships to fall to pieces by drawing out the nails and bolts."

† Abou-Zeid-Hassan writes a book supposed to contain the travels of a merchant named Soleyman, who describes the country of Zendj.

through their nostrils. There are men in these countries covered with skins who, stick in hand, advance to habitations and preach to the people. A century afterwards Albyrouny* writes of a commerce between Sofala, India, and China which had enriched a city named Soumenat. Then comes Edrisi, a geographer of the twelfth century. He tells us that El Banes is the nearest dependency on the coast of Zendj to Sofala. Near this is a great mountain which draws towards it all the vessels which approach, and therefore navigators have to avoid it carefully. The town of Tehnet also depends on the country of Sofala. "In all Zendj the principal productions are iron and the skins of the tigers of Zanguebar. . . . The Zendj people have at heart a great respect for the Arabs; that is why, when they see an Arab, be he traveller or merchant, they prostrate themselves before him, exalt his dignity, and say to him in their language, 'Be welcome to us, O Son of Yemen.'" In the description of Sofala we are told that villages are there similar to those of the

* See "Fragments Arabes et Persanes," par M. Reinaud, p. 112.

Arabs named *Djentama* and *Dendema*. They are situated upon the shores of the sea, and are inconsiderable. The inhabitants are miserably poor and have no resource but that obtained from iron. "There exists a great number of mines of this metal in the mountains of Sofala." One of the towns of this country is named Siouna, whose population is composed of Indians, people of Zendj, and others. "In all the country of Sofala they find gold in abundance and of excellent quality. Nevertheless the inhabitants prefer copper and make ornaments of it." Writing of the towns of Djesta and Djebesta it is said, "They find gold in quantity—working for it is the sole industry and the only resource of the inhabitants. . . . The town of Daghouta is the last of Sofala, country of gold; it is situated upon a great gulf; its inhabitants go naked. The women have the modesty not to show themselves because of their nudity, this is why they stay at home. . . . This country touches that of Ouac-Ouac, where are miserable towns. . . . In this neighbourhood is a big town named Dargha or Daghdagha, where the natives are black, of hideous figure, and deformed complexion: their language is a species of hissing. They go absolutely naked, and are little visited by strangers; they live on fish, shell fish, and tortoises. . . . Sofala and Ouac-Ouac produce much gold, and are at the termination of ship voyages from Oman and Syraf."

Ibn Sayd,[*] an Arab geographer who wrote about the middle of the thirteenth century, supplies us with an extraordinary description of Africa as far south as the Cape of Good Hope. According to him a desert existed between the country of Zendj and Sofala. He calls the latter a country of gold, and speaks of the cities of Banyna and Syouna. He takes care to repeat the warning to be found in other grave authors about the dangers of the loadstone mountain which, according to the "Thousand and One Nights," proved the destruction of Sindbad. He tells us that, "The King of Sofala resides at

[*] "Introduction a la Geographie d'Aboulfeda," par M. Reinaud, S. 11, p. 141. In reality the description of Africa only seems to be as far south as Cape Corrientes. Ibn Sayd says that the Nile takes its source from the Lake of Koura under the equinoctial line, and from the mountain El-Moquecem.

Syouna. The original inhabitants of this country, like those of Zendj, adore idols of wood and of stone, which they anoint with oil obtained from large fish. The most of the utensils which they use are of iron and of gold. They clothe themselves in the skins of tigers. They have no horses, and their people travel entirely on foot. El Masoudi reports that the Zendj people make war mounted on their oxen, as Nubians fight upon their dromedaries. . . . At the foot of the mountain El - Nedama and upon the canal* of Comr is the town of Daghouta, the last of the country of Sofala, and the last of the inhabited places in the lands which border this sea." A treatise on geography composed by Zakaria-ben-Mohammed or El-Cazouyny, which followed that of Ibn Sayd, is even less explicit, and gives us no additional information. Aboulfeda, however, lived about the same time, and his treatises are so celebrated that he has been styled the Prince of Geography. Writing of the works of this

---

* The Mozambique Channel was styled a canal. Any passage between an island and the mainland seems to have been called by the same name.

great authority, M. Guillain is compelled to say that, so far as Eastern Africa is concerned, Aboulfeda seems almost to copy Ibn Sayd, and does not increase our knowledge. In his introduction, however, he passes in review the Mahometan writers who were his contemporaries, specially naming Schems-Eddin, Nowairi, Omary, Ibn-el-Ouardy, and Hamd-Allah. These men wrote in the middle of the thirteenth and beginning of the fourteenth centuries. M. Reinaud informs us that from the middle of the fourteenth century to the end of the fifteenth only two Arab works on geography were written—one in 1403, by Abd-er-Rachid-ben-Saleh, surnamed El Bakoui, entitled "Summary of the Monuments and Wonders of the All-powerful King," while the other, written by Abd-el-Rassai, surnamed El-Samarkandy, is entitled "The Rise of Two Favourable Stars and the Reunion of Two Seas." We are told in this that, "To the great isle of the country of Zendj, where their king resides, all the vessels which come to trade resort. There are vines there which bear fruit three times in the year." But a great stimulus was given to geographical research when it was possible to read in Europe the voyages of the Venetian Marco Polo and those of the native of Morocco named Abou-Abd-Allah Mohammed. It was seen also that riches were to be obtained by commerce in the southern hemisphere. To open up a trade to India became the hope of every navigator, and even Columbus only discovered a continent in his endeavour to find a new path to one of the well-known portions of the ancient world.

There were no doubt important towns on the littoral of South-eastern Africa dominated by Mahometan Arabs. At one time we are told that Quiloa possessed the monopoly of the rich trade in the gold of Sofala. In all books not only is the country inland from Sofala declared to be auriferous, but the mines are invariably stated to be very rich. Two means were in all ages evidently used to obtain the precious metal. One was that of mining by shafts in the Phœnician fashion, extracting the gold quartz, crushing it and washing out the gold. The other is the process still going on of washing the golden sands of certain rivers and obtaining the "dust," referred to so many ages back in one of the oldest books of the Sacred Scriptures—that of Job. It must be admitted that some degree of skill is absolutely necessary for successful gold mining, and it is evident that so imperfect was the knowledge as well as the appliances of ancient ages, that the quartz treated must have been remarkably rich. Great workings remain, but the mines were not exhausted; indeed, in many cases, it will probably be found that only a commencement was made. Great tracts of auriferous country are now being explored, and the extraordinary quantity of old shafts and pits proves to what an extent at one time this source of wealth was attended to. It is certainly a startling fact, illustrating the truth of the aphorism that there is "nothing new under the sun," when we find what was very probably the mines of Ophir one thousand years before Christ, become the most recent "diggings" of the British South Africa Company, in the reign of Queen Victoria.

The people who went to Ophir in the fleet manned by Hebrews and Jews, which sailed from Ezion-Geber in the reign of King Solomon, found gold ready from the mines for export. Whether or not any of them joined their fortunes to those of the people in the country cannot be told, but it is almost certain that previously men of Phœnician extraction had penetrated into the auriferous regions and taught the art of mining, as well as the tenets of their litholatrous Nature worship. Of all the people of antiquity they were the miners *par excellence*—skilled in the art of extracting and working ores. The Arabs were not skilled in this direction, but may have gone to the forts in Monomotapa. There can be little question but that both Phœnician and Arab settlers merged themselves into the population by intermarriage. The Mashonas still use on their pottery the fretwork pattern significant of Phœnician times and Phœnician monuments and worship. The exact same markings are found both in Sardinia and in South-eastern Africa. The great vicissitudes of the world do not seem to have materially affected the mixed race which dwelt around the ancient forts. Their country was fertile and their wants simple. The luxury which the use of their gold promoted seems to have been relegated to other climes. In the absence of any record we have to consult the histories in stones which have been left us and the less reliable stories of the Arabian geographers. The work is necessarily of an eminently unsatisfactory character, as it merely represents a species of groping after truth. Everything around is dark, and the mere distant and uncertain glimmerings of light which we can perceive may frequently lead us in a wrong direction. The greatest indulgence, therefore, is justly due to an effort of exploration in a comparatively new direction, regarding, as it does, so difficult a problem as the partial solution of the questions raised in the discovery of the African Sphynxes of the modern world.

BOOK III.

PORTUGAL.

THE nephew of King Henry IV. of England and the great-grandson of Edward III., the famous Prince Henry of Portugal, surnamed the Navigator, was the principal agent in pushing forward those enterprising voyagers who at last succeeded in doubling the Cape of Good Hope and thus finding a new way to the Indies. In small vessels intrepid Portuguese mariners dared to venture upon unknown seas,* and at last the Cape of

* The most absurd narratives of dangers in the Southern Ocean existed. For instance, Ibn Khaldun, at the end of the fourteenth century, informs the world that the "Atlantic was a vast and boundless ocean, on which ships dare not venture out of sight of land, for even if the sailors knew the direction of the winds, they would not know whither those winds would carry them, and as there is no inhabited country beyond, they would run great risk in being lost in mist and vapour." The

Storms was reached by Bartholomew Diaz in the year 1498. An ardent desire of discovery, the propagation of Christianity, but, above all, the wish to obtain a large share of the great Eastern trade and extend the power of Portugal, animated the breasts of the rulers of that country and of the daring and enterprising sailors whom they sent.

The extraordinary stories about Prester John, monarch of Ethiopia, induced the King of Portugal to endeavour both by land and sea to discover his great empire. Pedro de Covilham and Affonso de Payva were sent to Aden *viâ* Naples, Rhodes, Alexandria, and Cairo. Payva subsequently went to Suakim, while his companion proceeded to India, but it was agreed that both should meet at Cairo. Subsequently Covilham passed over to Sofala on the South-eastern Coast of Africa, where he learned some particulars of the great gold mines of the interior, and at the same time

Geography of Ibn Sayd informs us that a Moor, named Ibn Fatimah, when wrecked near Cape Blanco, was warned not to go near it as "the whole of that mountain is one mass of deadly serpents. Strangers take it for a rock of glittering colour, and, deceived thereby, come near and are devoured by the serpents."

of the Island of the Moon, since known as Madagascar. When Covilham arrived at Cairo he heard of the death of his colleague, Payva, and met Rabbi Abraham, of Beja, and Joseph, of Lamego, by whom Covilham immediately despatched letters to King John of Portugal, in which he pointedly states, " that the ships which sail down the coast of Guinea might be sure of reaching the termination of the continent by persisting in a course to the south ; and that when they should arrive in the eastern ocean, their best direction must be to inquire for Sofala and the Island of the Moon." It is evident that King John was determined to use every effort in his power to open up new realms of adventure, riches, and commerce for the people of Portugal. It was the knowledge possessed by Rabbi Abraham and his companion of the Eastern spice trade which recommended them at Court, and induced the Government to send them not only in search of Covilham and Payva, but to go to the Persian coast and put themselves in a position to report as fully as possible on Eastern commerce. When Abraham proceeded to King John of Portugal,

Covilham travelled into Abyssinia, where he found such favour with the Negus as to be induced to remain permanently in the country. He married, occupied high posts, and amassed a fortune. Alvarez tells us that when in 1525 the Portuguese Ambassador, Don Rodriguez de Lima, arrived with his suite in Abyssinia, Covilham shed tears of joy at the sight of his countrymen. It is to this celebrated adventurer that has been assigned the honour of the theoretical discovery of the Cape of Good Hope, as his letter to King John clearly indicated where it was situated and how it could be reached.

Bartholomew Diaz, who set sail for the south with two vessels, each of fifty tons burthen, in August, 1486, performed one of the most heroic deeds which have ever been commemorated in any history. He was the gallant scion of a daring race of mariners. Joao Diaz had been one of the first to double Cape Boyador, and Deniz Diaz was among the foremost navigators who coasted Senegal and discovered Cape Verd. They went to explore unknown seas and to meet the greatest because the most unforeseen dangers. At this period it was customary to raise stone pillars as records of discovery, and when Diaz reached Pedestal Point on the West African Coast, one of these was erected. The cape at the mouth of the Orange River is called "Voltas," because contrary winds caused frequent tacks to be made, and from this point they were driven by violent gales, under reefed canvas, for no less than thirteen days, during which time they doubled the cape, as the first harbour into which they ran was Fleisch Bay, near the mouth of the Gouritz river, then called by them Vaqueiros, from the fact of cowherds having been observed on land at this place. Subsequently the Bay of San Bras was reached, where the natives made an attack, in repulsing which one of them was unfortunately slain by the Portuguese. This was greatly deplored, as the strictest injunctions had been given to propitiate the Aborigines. To carry out this plan a negress had been left at Angra Pequina and another at the mouth of the Orange river. Those women were well affected towards Portugal, and were expected to speak in praise of the Portuguese because of the kindness they had experienced from them. In this way possibly alliances with the natives of South Africa might be facilitated and information obtained such as that so much desired respecting Prester John. Algoa Bay was on this occasion nearly the terminal point of the voyage of Bartholomew Diaz. Here he erected a cross on the little island of St. Croix at the mouth of the Sundays River, and then desiring, like another Columbus, to push forward and discover an eastern world, he experienced such reproaches, and received such representations from his crew, that a compromise had to be effected, and the end of the voyage was reached when they cast anchor at the mouth of the Rio do Infanta, since known as the Great Fish River.*

* In tracing the events connected with the discovery and circumnavigation of the Cape of Good Hope our acknowledgments are due to the very precise and valuable work, "The Life of Prince Henry of Portugal, surnamed the Navigator, and its results, comprising the Discovery within one Century of half the World," by Richard Henry Major, F.S.A., F.R.S.L., &c., Keeper of the Department of Maps and Charts in the British Museum, and Hon. Sec. of the Royal Geographical Society, London, A. Asher & Co., 1868. M. Sourdade de Geographia de Lisboa has published a valuable work,

The earnest desire of discovering a new passage to the Indies which animated both Columbus and Diaz—Spain and Portugal—resulted, within a brief interval of five years, in the discovery of a new continent and of a new route to an old one. Ten years were allowed to elapse before a practical attempt was made to utilise the latter, and then an experienced navigator of noble family was chosen by King Manoel the Fortunate to command a small fleet of four vessels, the largest of which did not exceed one hundred and twenty tons burthen, whose destination was the East Indies *viâ* the Cape of Good Hope. Vasco da Gama anchored in the Bay

" Discobertas e Discobridores. De Como e quando foi feito Conde Vasco da Gama. Memoria apresentada a 10 Sessao do Congresso Internacional dos Orientalistos por Luciano," Cordeira S.S.G.L. (Secretary Society Geographical, Lisbon). We have also publicly to thank Sir Luciano Cordeira for copies of his works in French and Portuguese on the rule of Portugal in South-east Africa and on Monomotapa; also for other works forwarded by him—all of very great value and importance—largely utilised in this book, and which we hope to hand over to the Historical Library in the Archives of the Cape Colony. In Appendix D are pictures of certain Pillars erected by the Portuguese in South Africa.

of St. Bras on the 25th of November, 1497, and there encountered Hottentots whom he found it necessary to frighten, and erected a cross which was immediately thrown down by the natives. Subsequently, having visited Algoa Bay and called at the mouth of the Great Fish River, they discovered the land of Natal, and found there an entirely different people from any they had yet met. In spite of their large bows and iron-tipped assegais Da Gama established friendly relations with them. It was on Monday, January 22nd, that the fleet anchored in the Quillimane river at the mouth of the Zambesi, and there it is significant to learn they met Mahometan merchants from whom Da Gama gathered important information respecting the route to India. On the 10th of March the island of Mozambique was reached, where the people told them that Prester John (about whom the Portuguese were specially ordered to inquire) lived at an immense distance inland, but that he owned cities along the coast where there were many merchants and large ships. The vessels which the Portuguese actually did see were undecked and fastened by means of leather and without nails. The sails were made of palm leaves, but in spite of these primitive appliances the mariners possessed, and used, Genoese compasses as well as quadrants and charts. On the 7th of April another Moorish port, Mombasa, was reached, and there they experienced, but in a greater degree, the proverbial perfidy with which the Moors were always charged. Escaping, however, from all the traps that were laid, they eventually reached India successfully. On the return voyage no less than three months were occupied in reaching Africa, and there the Portuguese were received in a wonderfully friendly manner by the Sultan of the Moors at Melinda. At Mozambique a pillar was raised in testimony of the right to it acquired by the King of Portugal; they called at the Bay of St. Bras, and it was not until August, 1499, that Vasco da Gama reached Lisbon.

In the sixteenth century the chief commercial aspirations of Portugal tended towards India, while in the seventeenth century Brazil became the great subject of her hopes. Africa was thus comparatively neglected during both periods, and it certainly does not seem that any adequate means were ever adopted to thoroughly subjugate the country of Monomotapa and to utilise the great gold mines which were undoubtedly known to exist there. The mysterious silence of the Arabians for centuries was explained when the nature and character of their trade for gold at Sofala was discovered, and shortly after Da Gama's visit to the coast information about them roused the attention, the cupidity, and the activity of the Portuguese. A year after Da Gama's return Pedro Alvarez Cabral* was charged with the command of an expedition to Calicut. Da Gama was again sent out with ten ships in 1502. In the next year (1503) Antonia de Saldanha went with a small fleet to India, but it was not until the year 1503 that King Manoel sent fifteen ships bearing fifteen thou-

* Bartholomew Diaz, the discoverer of the Cape, sailed in this fleet. We are told that "The fleet set sail on the 22nd of May. . . . The appearance of an immense comet produced an alarm which was only too unhappily realised. A fearful typhoon sunk four vessels, and the brave Bartholomew Diaz, whose great achievements had converted his stormy cape into a Cape of Good Hope, perished off that very cape which for him was still to be a Cape of Storms" (Major's "Prince Henry the Navigator," p. 410).

sand men under the command of Don Francesco de Almeida, first Viceroy of the Indies, with specific instructions to commence practical operations in Africa by building fortresses at Sofala and Quiloa. The war with the Moors of the South-eastern Coast definitely began; Quiloa was captured, while the King of Sofala was made tributary to Portugal, and a fort was built there. In 1506 the Viceroy ordered Vasco Gomez de Abreu to erect the first fortifications at Mozambique for which larger and finer buildings were substituted in 1545. Lorenço Marques* explored Delagoa Bay and there can be no doubt that the coast of East Africa, in many important places, was occupied by Portugal. The Moors had to succumb to the power of European arms, and both trade and mineral treasures to a great extent passed out of their hands.

Sofala was the new gold coast. Of this there could be no doubt. The testimonies are numerous and ample from the books of

* The results of observations made by the Portuguese are summarised by Mesquito Perestrello in his "Itinerary of Ports, Marine Routes, Heights, Capes, Soundings, &c., from the Cape of Good Hope to Cape Corrientes, 1575." Again in "L'Arte de Navigar, Manuel Pimental," 1681.

Duente Barbosa, Santos, and many others. One of the most valuable works about South-eastern Africa is three volumes in folio containing the letters of Fathers of the Society of Jesus, originally owned by the College of Evora and now preserved in the Library of the Royal Academy of Sciences of Lisbon.* Tome Lopez, who was a clerk in the ship of Mendez de Vasconcellos, wrote a description of part of South-east Africa which is preserved in the collection of Ramusio. He tells us that as they arrived at the mouth of the Sofala river when the sea was calm they were able to anchor, and that subsequently they observed various villages, the people of which invited them to enter. The admiral received gold there, and the remark is made that the Moors were careful never to show the precious metal for fear this should incite

---

* A translation of this great work would be of immense advantage. In the first folio volume the letters are principally from Japan, while in the second are those sent to his superiors by Father Silveira the South African proto-martyr. Valuable extracts from these are contained in a Portuguese work recently published by Sir Luciano Cordeira, and to be given to the Archives Historical Library of the Cape Colony.

Christians to enter the country. This early chronicler tells us that King Solomon received gold here. Subsequently at Mozambique, when he questioned the Moors about the mines, they answered that certainly a great war was raging in the countries of gold, and for that reason trade was then interrupted, but that in normal times of peace no less than two millions of *meligaes* were annually taken from the country in ships of India, Mecca, and other countries. Each one of these *meligaes* was worth a ducat and a half, so that if this statement be approximately accurate it is evident that even by primitive methods of working, the yield of the mines was considerable.* Duarte Barbosa was another clerk or supercargo who travelled with Magaelhans, and at one time was stationed in South-eastern Africa. His book was completed in 1516. He tells us that at Sofala there is a population of Arabs, and near them the King of Portugal had built a fortress. "Those Moors have a long time established themselves there because of their

* See "Colleccio de Noticias para a historiæ geographica das ultramarinos," tome ii. pp. 107, 161, 164.

great gold trade with the interior." He gives us to understand that large vessels came from Arabia to such a port as Quiloa, and thence small coast boats were employed to proceed to Sofala. He describes elaborately the stuffs —blue cotton cloths, &c., which took the fancy of the natives. "The people of Monomotapa come to Sofala charged with gold and give such quantities that the merchants gain 100 for 1. A great deal of ivory is also collected." The two ports of the coast to which the Portuguese paid special attention were Sofala, because of the gold and ivory trade, and Mozambique, because it was looked upon as a half-way house between the Cape of Good Hope and India, suitable for the refreshment of outward and homeward bound fleets. The capture of Quiloa, and the general defeat of the Arabs of the coast by the Portuguese, followed by the establishment of fortresses duly garrisoned had followed by commercial transactions. We read that in 1554 "greater part of the trade for India was taken at Sofala." The Portuguese began to establish themselves at various points on the Zambesi (Cuama) river, and we shall see that traders, missionaries, and military expeditions were eventually despatched from there. But no inland settlements worthy of the name were ever founded. The coast alone was held, and that by military occupation. The Portuguese, like all the Latin races, are really not colonisers. They can conquer and hold by means of troops, fight for dominion of provinces whose mineral treasures are of consequence; but to systematise emigration and induce the people brought out to make the new land their permanent home, and by degrees raise up civilisation and empire, are tasks which they seem never even to have seriously contemplated. In South-eastern Africa they have always been strangers in a strange land, retaining with difficulty coast acquisitions and never able to hold permanently the great and rich interior. The utmost praise is due, and should be given unreservedly, to the great mariners whose discoveries have thrown lustre upon the country which was so wise and adventurous as to send them forth. Their brave soldiers followed by bold deeds in the path of adventure, but although they have always claimed they have never been able to hold adequately the country of Monomotapa. No dog-in-the-manger policy is ever allowable on gold-fields. If a registered holder of a claim be unwilling or unable to work it, the first comer who is able to do so has a right to seize it and utilise its contents for his own benefit and that of the public. So with great countries — where there are minerals — the tide will flow towards them, and if the nominal owner be unable to subjugate savages who stop the way, the people who succeed in doing so consider that they have a right to the land.

Monomotapa is the great interior empire said by some writers to extend from Mozambique to the Cape of Good Hope. In reality it extended only between the Zambesi and Limpopo rivers, although it is possible that tributary kingdoms south of the Limpopo may have existed. Moenemugi was the empire north of the Zambesi. The most precise dimensions we have been able to discover in ancient Portuguese works place Monomotapa between 31° and 66° long. E., and 14° and 25° S. lat., from the Zambesi as far as to the river of Spiritu Sancto; this empire extended along the coast of the Indian Ocean for 960 miles. Monomotapa means lord of all, and this was the dominant empire to which many so-called kings were subject. The Arabs evidently had been content with trading facilities which by no means necessitated conquest, and the people of Monomotapa, who were evidently a mixed race, entirely different from the fierce barbarians who became to them what the Goths, Huns, and Lombards were to the people of Europe. Let us endeavour to discover the nature and character of the people of Monomotapa at the beginning of Portuguese dominion. Duarte Barbosa, writing very early in the sixteenth century, says: "In the interior (from Sofala), fifteen or twenty days' journey, is a great population named Zimbaohe, which has many houses of wood and straw. Among such people is very often the King of Benematapa.* In Beazento, where the king oftener lives, is a place very great where his merchants are bringing gold to Sofala, and they give this gold to the Moors without weighing it in exchange for stuffs highly valued by them.

* Benematapa or Monomotapa, signifying great lordships, are words used indiscriminately.

These Moors of Benematapa say that there is much gold in a country very far situated in the direction of the Cape of Good Hope, in another kingdom* which is subjected to this King of Benematapa—a very great lord having many kings under his vassalage. His country runs through the desert as far as from Mozambique to the Cape of Good Hope." In the historical description of the most wonderful countries of the world by Johnstone, published in 1603, we are supplied with a fair summary of what could then be learned from Portuguese writers. He tells us that, "In the residue of Ethiope raigne divers powerful princes as the Kings of Adell, Monomugi, Monomotapa, Angola, and Congo. Monomotapa is mightier and more famous than the rest. This kingdom containeth all that island which lieth between the river of Cuama and Spirito Santo (a territory of 150 leagues in compass), and from Spirito Santo it stretches to the Cape of Good Hope,

---

* Ancient workings in parts of the South African Republic show that gold mining took place there probably in prehistoric periods. So far the modern mines of the Transvaal—specially including those of Johannesburg—have proved to be the richest.

for the viceroys of that huge tract do acknowledge him for their sovereign and superior governor. The soil aboundeth with corn and cattle. By the store of teeth not less than 5,000 elephants must die yearly. Zimba and Benemaraxa are cities. There is no climate like it for plenty of gold, for by report there is 3,000 miles whereout gold is digged; gold is likewise found in the earth, in rocks, and in rivers. The mines of Manica, Boro, Quiticui, and Totoe (which some men call Butua) are the richest. The people are mean of stature, black, and well set. They converse with the king kneeling. The offences most punished are witchcraft, theft, and adultery. The king beareth on his coat of arms a certain little spade with an ivory handle, and two small darts. He keepeth for his faithfulest guard two hundred dogs. He keepeth the heirs of the vassal princes to be secured of their father's loyalty." " Purchas his Pilgrimage " is one of the most valuable books of reference so far as Monomotapa is concerned, as he gives copious references to Portuguese authorities. Not only, however, has he obtained all information which could then possibly be procured, but he is a judicious and candid critic. Nevertheless he is obliged to give the tales of the day and some of them certainly are sufficiently incredible. He informs us that the royal ensign of Monomotapa is a little ploughshare with an ivory point which the king always carried at his girdle. No prisoners were ever retained, and therefore there was no necessity for gaols. This plan of executing summary justice was eminently economical, and the trial by ordeal was used instead of trial by jury. Those charged with offences had frequently to swallow the bark of a certain tree, and if they vomited, the sentence of guilty was pronounced. If, however, no sickness resulted the accuser had to submit to the ordeal under the same conditions. Father Monteiro, S.J., says in one of his letters that on the banks of the Zambesi the subjects of Monomotapa when charged with crimes had to try to swim across that broad stream. If they were devoured by crocodiles on the passage then there could be no doubt about their guilt, whereas if they escaped these savage animals they also escaped all terrors of the law. Purchas duly informs us that the Emperor of Monomotapa had no fewer than one thousand wives, one of which only was principal; and then goes on quoting Johannes Boterus, to tell us that his chief warriors are women. "Certain Amazones which seare off their left paps lest they hinder their shooting." He is careful, however, to add, "For my part no Amazonian battle yet conquered my credit." We quote Purchas because he is one of those writers who collected in one focus all the information from Portuguese and other sources available. He speaks of other kingdoms adjoining to Monomotapa and the Mountains of the Moon, while he refers to the Hottentots of Southern Africa having "their necks adorned with chaines of greasy trypes." So far as the Quiteu or great ruler of Monomotapa was concerned his titles of honour were numerous. "They call the Quiteu by prodigious titles and specially entitle him 'Great'—as 'Great Thiefe,' 'Great Witch,' 'Great Lion.'" The races from the north had already penetrated far south, and the reports about them show how fierce and savage they were believed to be. "The Jagges are exceeding devourers of man's flesh, for which they refuse beef and goats. Each man has twenty wives and each child is buried when born. Their reason is that they will not be troubled with education. They bring up conquered native boys over ten. They wear a collar until they bring an enemy's head. If one run away he is killed and eaten. The Anzigues be the cruellest canniballs which the Sun looketh on, for in other places they eat their enemies or the dead, but here they take and eat their kinsfolkes. They keep shambles of man's flesh, as with us of beef and mutton. Some worshipped the greatest goates they could get—bats, owls, and screech owls." This language is significant, as it shows the reputation of the invading hordes whose barbarism did so much to stifle the imperfect civilisation of Monomotapa as well as to prevent the Portuguese ever gaining complete mastery over the country. When considering the nature and character of the people of Southeastern Africa, it is very desirable to refer to the pages of Santos, a Dominican monk, and to the letters of Fathers Silveira and Monteira, the Jesuits. In these narratives there is no attempt to exalt Monomotapa into a wonderfully civilised empire ruled over by a monarch, the walls of whose houses were plated by gold. Some Portuguese writers indulge in absurdly inflated descriptions, but the truth is that the original people of the Zimbabwes comprised a race which was mixed certainly, but only to a small extent, the negroid element being far in the ascendant. Intermixture with other African races no doubt reduced them to a lower level than they had been for many hundreds of years after the forts were built. The Mashonas no doubt are descendants of the people of Monomotapa, but persecuted, down-trodden, hunted, and mercilessly murdered for generations. Those of them in comparatively unexposed portions of country where they were less liable to Zulu incursions, give us an idea of what their forefathers were. They understand how to extract gold from quartz, are expert smiths and workers in metal, cultivate the land with some skill and considerable industry, while their manners are comparatively refined. They are not warlike, still live in the straw huts their ancestors built, and have among them on their pottery, etc., the exact fretwork decorations typical of the Phœnician litholatrous worship practised countless ages ago.

It is difficult to say that we have yet completely gauged the religious feelings and opinions of the Mashonas. No doubt by degrees they have adopted spiritualism or worship of ancestors universally practised around, but in tradition there must still be some lingering remains of that Nature and stone worship believed in by the men who built the Zimbabwe forts in ancient times. Mr. Theodore Bent, when quoting Santos, says, "He told no lies, and any one who has been among the inhabitants as they now are will recognise in his narrative a faithful and accurate account of the people, proving how little they have altered in the lapse of between three and four centuries."* Santos † tells us that the country was greatly split up in consequence of one of the Monomotapa or chief

---

* "Ruined Cities of Mashonaland," p. 201.

† "Santos Jean dos (Dominican) Primeira parte de Ethiopia Oriental, em que se da relacem dos principaes reynos desta regias dos costumes, ritos et abusos de seas habitadores, dos animaes, bichos et feras . . . de varios querras entre christianos Mauros et Gentios." Evora, Manuel de Lira, 1602, 2 part, in 1 vol. in folio. There is a translation of this work into French by R. P. Don Gaetau Charpy, Paris, 1684.

rulers having sent three sons to govern the provinces of Quiteve, Sedanda, and Chicanga, who permanently retained the power thus conferred on them in their respective families, so that including the direct descendant of the great monarch four kingdoms arose in the country. But subsequent subdivisions took place and the country thus became a more easy prey to the Zulu invader. The present native people of the Zimbabwe countries call themselves Makalangas. Dos Santos, quoted by Mr. Bent, says: "The Monomotapa and all his vassals are Mocarangas, a name which they have because they live in the land of Mocaranga, and talk the language called Mocaranga, which is the best and most polished of all Kafir languages which I have seen in this Ethiopia." These children of the sun, as their name signifies, were probably originally a branch of the great invading Bantu race. They came into Monomotapa, mixed with the people, and for centuries ruled over the country until more powerful and fierce invaders subdued them in their turn. Certainly they must have taken wives in the country of their adoption, as the mixed race living near the Zimbabwes has been, so far as metal work, agriculture, and the arts of peace are concerned, quite contradistinguished from the fierce and brutal warriors of Moselekatze and Lo Bengulo. When Dos Santos describes the people of Monomotapa of the sixteenth century, he describes the Mashona people of the present day. They had an indistinct idea of a Supreme Being, and held feasts in honour of their ancestors. They smelted iron and their workmen made good spears, assegai heads, and mattocks. Kafir beer was their principal drink, men and women used bracelets for their arms and legs, made curious pianos with iron rods enclosed in pumpkins, and celebrated as holy "Mozimos" or days of the holy dead.

It may be interesting to note what is said by one of the greatest Venetian authorities on the subject of Monomotapa. Livio Sanuto published his "Geographia dell Africa" in Venice in 1588. He says Benomotapa is ruled over by a prince called by this proper name for Emperor. The country is embraced like an island by two arms of a river which proceeds from the same lake whence the Nile and Zaire take their source. The country has a circuit of about three thousand miles, and there are many rivers in which there is gold. If the people sought in earnest after gold they would obtain it in great quantities, but they only take it to suit their fancy, or to give them the means of buying from foreigners. They worship a single god " Mozimo," and have no idols. Death is the penalty for idolatry and adultery. The Emperor has as many wives as he pleases, but the son of the principal wife inherits. They offer food to the dead, and collect the bones of the deceased after the flesh has fallen away from them. They wear cotton clothing worked with gold thread. The King of Monomotapa holds sway to the Cape of Good Hope, and great gifts are given to him by subject kings. Gifts are carried on the heads of bearers to the palace. This monarch keeps five hundred buffoons. Among his soldiers there are five thousand women who fight. He sends people round every year to put out fires, and then gives them a new light. Any one interfering with this arrangement is put to death. One day's labour in thirty is given to the king. Trial by ordeal takes place, when a certain berry mixed with water is given to the accused, and if he vomit after drinking he is found guilty. Two hundred dogs are kept by the king. In the midst of the ancient mines that are known, Zimbaoe stands. Here is a fortress made of rough stones. Above the gate is an inscription after the fashion of an epitaph which no one has been able to understand. The word Zimbaoe signifies Court, and any place where Benomotapa goes is called so. They give the custody of this fortress to a nobleman, as they do in Castile. These buildings are supposed to have been built to keep the gold. The mines now have not been worked for many years, by reason of the wars. Ptolemy calls the place Agesemba, and there is supposed to be a place like it in a plain of the Pretegeanni called Caxumo, which is said to be a city of the Queen of Saba, which Ptolemy calls Auxuma. There is great trouble experienced in getting gold from Manica, because of the absence of water.

It is desirable to quote a writer like Sanuto, as he had exceptional facilities for obtaining information. His work was intended to embrace the four quarters of the world, but he died when only one of them, "Africa," was completed. We referred to a beautiful copy, excellently printed on good paper, in the Barberini Library, Rome. In the same library is a MS. memorial to the Pope, written in 1603, referring to the progress of the Church in Ethiopia—in the southern portion of which Monomotapa was deemed to be. Father Silveira's work is alluded to, and it is said that it is very difficult to enter Ethiopia because of the difficulties of the mountains and people, who are cannibals. Looking at the matter in a temporal point of view they could bring all these countries at a small expense under European control—Tigre and Doncala excepted—the whole country being very rich. Monomotapa was in one of the fourteen Missionary provinces into which Pope Innocent XII. divided the world.

De Barros in his "Decades" gives us an account of early operations of Portugal on the shores of the Indian Ocean, and it is thus that he speaks of Sofala: "This territory forms part of a vast country over which a prince named Benomotapa rules. It is girdled so as to make it like an island by two arms of a great river (the Limpopo and Zambesi are meant), which takes its source in the greatest lake of Africa, where ancient geographers place the source of the Nile, and from which also the river Zaire flows which traverses the Congo. . . . The river of Sofala divides into two branches; the one falls into the sea at Cape Corrientes, and has taken successively the name of the river of the lake (De la goa) and of the river of the Holy Ghost. The other falls into the sea twenty-five leagues to the north of Sofala. This is the Cuama, named in the interior Zambesi. This branch is much more considerable than the other; it is navigable more than two hundred and fifty leagues; it receives six remarkable rivers, which bear the following names: Panhamca, Louamgona, Arrouya, Manjouo, Inadire, and Rouenia. All water the land of Monomotapa, and the most of them carry gold. The kingdom of Sofala is about seven hundred and fifty leagues in circuit, and resembles Zanguebar in its aspect, the animals which are found there, the men who inhabit it, and the food products which feed them. As the country of Sofala is well peopled, elephants take refuge in the solitudes of Zanguebar, where they travel in great troops. The mines of gold nearest to Sofala are those which bear the name of Manica; they are situated in a valley surrounded by an amphitheatre of mountains, thirty leagues in circuit. All this territory is named Matouca, and the people who extract the precious metal are the Botongas. The mines further away from Sofala are between one hundred and two hundred miles distant."

Here De Barros tries to grasp the idea of quartz crushing, but expresses himself far more picturesquely than exactly. He says that sometimes two hundred men are employed to use immense quantities of water in order to discover "the vase and the gold which it encloses." The earth is so rich that if the inhabitants were greedy "they could obtain enormous quantities of the precious metal, but they are so lazy, and have so few wants, that they require to be pushed by famine before they will work in the mines." In order to increase their covetousness, the Moors show them such rich and beautiful stuffs and ornaments as to excite their admiration and cause them to buy them on credit. "Take them," say the Moors, "seek for gold, and pay us on our return." They never failed in their engagements, and to accomplish this object were obliged to work the mines. The most ancient shafts were situated in a district named Taroa, in the kingdom of Batoua, and here it is where the great Zimbaoe, or King's Palace, or rather the ruins of it, were situated.

The description of De Barros is evidently a second-hand one, and too much credence cannot be given to the statement that "Upon the gate of this monument is an inscription which Moors and learned men who have visited the place are not able to read." He adds, "When and by whom were these edifices constructed? As writing is unknown among the people of the country, no information on the subject is preserved among them." Conjectures respecting the origin and destination of these great buildings may, he says, naturally be made. The Moors attribute a great antiquity to them, but no tradition reporting upon their origin exists. Then our author goes on to describe the people of the country, who, although blacks with woolly hair, are said to have more intelligence than the inhabitants of the Mozambique, Kiloua, and Melinde coasts. He says that there are cannibals among them, one of whose customs is to kill cattle for the purpose of drinking their blood. "Those of Benomotapa are very much disposed to be converted to Christianity. In fact, they believe in one god whom they name Mezimo, and they adore no idol, in opposition to the customs of all the other black people, who are idolaters and fetichists. Among them witchcraft (fetichism) is an abomination, and punished with death. They are not less severe against theft and adultery." The men were polygamists, having as many wives as they were able to support, the first being the principal, whom all the others were obliged to serve. The dress of the people is mostly made of imported cottons, but in many cases women and men of high rank wore silken robes embroidered with gold. The Benomotapa, or Emperor, however, never wears any clothes but those made in his country, lest something noxious to him might be introduced if they were obtained from abroad. Women are specially objects of veneration, and even th Emperor yields precedence to them.*

Youceuf, the Arab commandant at Sofala d made himself independent of the Arab ruler of Quiloa, and, as we have seen, permitted the Portuguese to erect a fort. Six ships under the command of Da Nhaya were sent by King Emmanuel of Portugal to operate on the South-eastern Coast of Africa, and by means of this force little difficulty was experienced in defeating the Arabs at Sofala and taking possession of the place. A proclamation was shortly afterwards issued forbidding the Moors to traffic here, which naturally caused the greatest possible dissatisfaction. At an early period Quiloa was occupied, and the "Sultans" there placed in a state of vassalage. With most creditable energy Portugal sent out fleets. In 1506 fourteen vessels quitted the Tagus with Alfonso du Albuquerque, but under the supreme com-

---

* Of course De Barros had to take his facts second-hand, and is no doubt frequently wrong. Dos Santos seems more reliable. More detailed information can be obtained in "Memoria æstatistica sobre os dominios Portuguezes na Africa Oriental," Lisbon, 1835.

mand of Tristan da Cunha. A few vessels were stationed for some time at Sofala, and others at Mozambique. Taking advantage of disputes among the Moors, several towns on the coast were captured with comparative ease.

This was the era of Portuguese greatness. Not only was the South-eastern Coast of Africa subdued, but Portugal carried her victorious arms to India, and even to China. Brave and skilful mariners, undaunted soldiers, and able commanders, made her the foremost maritime power of the day. Her sailors first doubled the Cape, entered Indian seas, and enjoyed the benefits of the riches not only of Calicut and Goa, but of Ceylon, the Moluccas, China, and Japan as well as of Sofala and of Monomotapa. An able and well-informed French writer speaks thus of Portugal: "It is not certainly without reason that all historians have looked with astonishment upon this colossal Portuguese domination extending from the Atlantic Ocean to the shores of China, founded in hardly the space of sixty years by the efforts of a people remarkable in Europe only for the smallness of their territory. A conquest notable both for its immensity and rapidity, and which would produce upon the mind of a philosopher an impression without analogy, if the destruction which followed it had not been as prompt and complete, for we are able to say at present that the abasement of that nation has been equal to its grandeur. . . . From one century to another the breath of events has levelled the giant edifice as if it had been made of sand, and history will only recount to people the marvels of its past." *

It is undesirable, and it would certainly be uninteresting to load this work with petty details connected with wars, intrigues, and conquests. Suffice it to say that the rule of Portugal became paramount on the Southeastern Coast of Africa, her prospectors and traders commenced to ascend the Zambesi and establish stations, commercial relations were even to some extent opened with Monomotapa, and the gold of Ophir which had flowed into the coffers of Solomon began to enrich the treasury of Portugal. The head-

* M. Guillain, Documents, " L'Afrique Orientale," première partie, p. 375.

quarters of Portuguese dominion in the Indian Ocean was fixed at Goa, and four great governments were placed under the sway of the viceroys stationed there. One of these was on the Eastern Coast of Africa,* where in a short time Quiloa and the fortress of Mozambique were abandoned to centralise power at Sofala, which was the most important place. In 1559 Goa was erected into an archbishopric endowed with primatial power. At this time Portuguese Jesuits reached there, following upon the footsteps of Saint Francis Xavier, and the people of South-eastern Africa naturally looked in that direction for missionaries.

It must be admitted that the Portuguese were eminently a Christian nation, and that invariably one of the real objects they had in view was the extension and promotion of Christianity. This was so much ostensibly one of their objects that the Popes gave Portugal all the facilities in their power, and

* The others were (1) Malacca in the island of that name; (2) the citadel and town of Hormuz, dominating the Portuguese possessions in the Persian Gulf; and (3) the island of Ceylon.

in the name of Christianity and for the purpose of its promotion accorded grants of territory in various parts of the world. A study of copies of letters from the Popes preserved in the Vatican will show that these were scarcely of the character and description which some Portuguese writers lead us to imagine.

By leave of the authorities of the Vatican Archives a thorough search was made for documents bearing reference to Africa, with the result that a list of about twenty letters was drawn up. Most of these, however, referred to Northern Africa. The letter quoted above, *apropos* to the grant of the Canary Islands, is interesting. It is a curious fact not generally known, that letters received at the Vatican were for a long period of time not preserved, but copies of letters from the Holy See have always been kept. The following is a translation of an interesting letter from Pope Urban VIII. to one of the converted monarchs of South-eastern Africa:
"To Hieronymus Tangovin, King of Mombasa and Melinde, Son much beloved in Christ, health and apostolical benediction.

Though the people of the kingdoms of this earth may revere the majesty of rulers with homage and tribute, nevertheless this is quite unable to procure for their hearts either peace in this world or happiness in the next. Unhappy kings have reason to tremble among their deceitful flatterers; virtue, not might, follows them on their way to eternity. The service of God is a kingdom, and God is so rich in mercy that while mortals obey them whom they fear, He, who has no want of our goods, complies with the will of His reverers. You are very happy, because you will be able now to extend to the heavenly country the kingdoms of your forefathers if you will truly fear God. No doubt the people who live happily under authority receive your orders with alacrity, but the Almighty Himself will submit His will to a king who serves God. Much beloved Son in Jesus Christ, we congratulate your Majesty upon this happiness. To your kingly heart has shone forth the light of the Holy Ghost, while through the salutary waters of baptism you have been able to come into the blissful port of Hope. While you submitted yourself and your power to

Christ and to the blessed Peter, who is always living in the Roman Pontiffs, you were called into the adoption of the sons of God, into the inheritance of the eternal Sovereignty. . . . From the Eastern African shores the fame of your piety has been wafted to this land. This will cause the blessing of Christianity to triumph, if by your authority and care you will prevail upon the princes of your nation to follow the pious example of their king. But against such enterprises the might of Hell, which is the enemy of your glory, will not fall asleep. Impious tongues will not be wanting which will try to remove your Majesty from such felicity. Be strong in the Lord; collect your forces. Dangers never turned the great Emperor Constantine aside —a name the boast both of East and West —who attained the glorious position of introducing Christ Himself, the King of kings, into the possession of the Roman Empire. Throw yourself into the field against the Prince of Darkness and Heaven will help you; Christ will help you; Christ will arm His crowned king with the shield of goodwill, a two-edged sword, and the helmet of salvation. The blessed Augustine himself—the bright light of your Africa and the whole Church—makes his voice thrill through your ears by means of the Augustinian missionaries, who seek in your kingdom the kingdom of God, and will assure you happiness. Believe, we pray, that these priests are sent as much from the heavenly country as from the Roman Church, in order that the impiety of your kingdom may be cast aside. By all benefits you will confer on them you will secure the love of Europe and the protection of Heaven. Beloved Son, we hope very much that with the blessing of Christ we will be able soon to change exhortations into glorious praises; and now we give you very heartily our paternal and apostolical blessing." As Gregory the Great sent Augustinian monks to England, so were these religions despatched by Innocent VIII. to South-east Africa. The seed was the same in each case, but the ground on which it fell was very different.

One of them, referring specially to the Canary Islands, points out reservations and special stipulations which puts the original grant in a light evidently not perceived, or at least admittted, by the King of Portugal. But it is not necessary to refer fully to this subject, as any contention for ownership founded upon Papal grants has long since disappeared. The active desire of spreading Christianity certainly animated the breasts of the Portuguese, and so eager were the people of Monomotapa to procure missionaries that earnest prayers for assistance were forwarded to Goa. At last, in response to these, the designate Jesuit Provincial at Goa, Father Silveira, with two other priests, were despatched to South-eastern Africa in the year 1559. The letters sent to Goa from Africa by these missionaries* have never yet been published in English, and extracts from them will be found interesting. In February, 1560, we find Father Silveira at Mozambique, making preparations for freighting an Asian boat, as he styles it, to take him to Sofala. He believes that the mission to Monomotapa may become very successful. We are told that the first place where they preached was

* They are contained in the collection of letters from Jesuits originally in the College of Evora, and now in the Royal Library, Lisbon.

in Tongue, within the kingdom of Gamba. Here they were hospitably received, and "the King of Tongue" expresses great satisfaction at receiving a letter from the Portuguese Viceroy of the Indies. Every inhabitant of the country who desired to become a Christian had free permission to embrace the faith, and the king himself in an incredibly short space of time determined to be baptised. The place in which all this occurred is stated to have been a minor kingdom. The ruler was evidently only a Kafir chief, for Father Fernandes says in one of his letters: "This king, for a Kafir, is very good and well-inclined. He is tall, discreet, and beloved by his neighbours." His country is declared by Father Silveira to be, as far as he can judge, "the most barren in the province, but the people are the best because they all belong to the tribe of the Mokarangas, who are reported better than the Bongoe, and Kaffraria is principally peopled by these two tribes."

From the letters which Father André Fernandes * wrote from Imhambane to

---
* See above collection.

Brother Luis Froes and to Fathers and
Brothers in the College of Goa during 1560,
we glean the following. In this country the
dews are very abundant, the lands are flat
and well watered, while there is much poultry,
very many fine cows, but fewer goats and
sheep. At Tongue the king was very much
astonished to see Father Fernandes, who
was an old man, travelling on foot, and
invited him to rest in his country. In fact,
he was very kind, and there seemed no difficulty in converting this Kafir chief and many
of his tribe to Christianity. Later on in
the year Father Silveira writes: "Thanks
be to God and to the Holy Virgin, the Queen
of Tongue, as well as the king's sons and
daughters, his household court and relations
—in a word, all the subjects of that kingdom
are now Christians. . . . On my way from
Tongue to the spot where I was to sail for
Mozambique I have baptised many chiefs or
little kings. Those of Tongue are Mocarangas."
He tells us that they have superstitions, but
no idolatry, therefore their conversion to the
Christian faith is much easier. It is thirty
leagues distant from Imhambane to Tongue,

which latter place is the metropolis of Gamba. "I am going alone to Monomotapa, where the devil, it is said, is making many conquests."

We now come to a letter written by Brother Balthasar da Costa, in India, to a Father of the Society of Jesus in Portugal, dated November 16, 1560. He states that after the conversion of the king and nation of Imhambane, including, of course, Gamba, Father André Fernandes and Brother André da Costa remained among them to confirm all in their new faith. Meanwhile Father Silveira had set forth alone to another kingdom, named Monomotapa, far greater than the first, "with the hope to lead this second king to the true knowledge of our Lord."

We have long descriptions of country, climate, customs of the people and superstitions, but virtually all this information is contained in the pages of Dos Santos and of De Barros. It is perfectly clear that the people styled as "Kafirs" dominated the country. Such grandiloquent titles as Emperor, King, Queens, and Princes, are perfect misnomers. The old race of Monomotapa had been completely swallowed up in the Makarangas, and the religion of the people who built their fortresses was as much destroyed and passed out of use as the great edifices constructed by them. Strange to say, we cannot even find any traditions unless of a most obscure and doubtful character. They, however, still used on their pottery a pattern linking them with the litholatrous Phœnicians and Arabians of the past, but they were really Kafirs. The domination of the black invader was complete, although it must be admitted that the Makarangas and their descendants, the Mashonas, of modern times were one of the mild and superior races of the South-east African continent. They tilled the land with some skill, were able to extract gold from quartz, and were not inexpert workers in metal. Nevertheless they lived in huts and gazed upon the colossal ruins of the Phœnicians as the works of strangers from whose religion and comparative civilisation they were alienated. It is easy to understand how such a vast transition could take place in a far inland region where hordes of barbarians penetrated. We cannot trace the progress of this movement, although it is easy, from the documents of the sixteenth century in our possession, to record its results.

The more the letters of the Jesuits and Dominicans are studied, the more apparent it becomes that all Monomotapa was what we can describe as a purely Kafir country. Father André Fernandes tells us that the permission to speak to a chief cannot be obtained without a present. Bocarro also refers to this constant custom. Worship of spirits of ancestors, witch doctors, absence of idolatry, and other salient customs are fully referred to; but we have already given adequate quotations, and would only be guilty of tiresome repetition if we were to publish fuller particulars contained in this correspondence.

Father Silveira is the proto-martyr of Monomotapa, indeed of South-eastern Africa, and his labours, sufferings, and death form the most glorious chapter in the Portuguese history of that country.* Sprung from a

* The chief sources of the information we are able to present to our readers respecting this martyr are: "Vita Patris Gonzali Sylveriæ, Societatis Jesu Sacerdotis. In Urbem Monomotapa martyrium passi. Lugduni Sumptibus Horatio Cardon, 1612." This book is written by Father Nicholas Godigno, and dedicated to the Father-

noble family, near Lisbon, he desired to follow in the footsteps of St. Francis Xavier in the East, and was ordered to the headquarters of civilisation in India, at Goa, where he soon was chosen to be Provincial. Letters arrived earnestly asking for missionary aid in South-eastern Africa, and we have already seen that in response to them he went with two other Fathers of this Society to Inhambane and succeeded in converting the king or chief of Gamba, residing at Tongue. Subsequently he had to travel great distances. Leaving Mozambique in September, 1560, he sailed to the river Mafute, but on the way encountered a very violent storm in which all were in imminent danger of perishing, when, we are informed, in answer to the prayers of Silveira,

General Claudius Aquaviva, from whom there is a decree of approbation, dated December 8, 1611. We give in the Appendix a translation of the account of the death of Father Silveira, extracted from this scarce book. The contemporary letters of Fathers of the Society, specially letters from Brother Luis Froez, written in 1561 and to be found in the great collection of correspondence already referred to in the Royal Library of Lisbon. The great "History of the Society of Jesus," by Orlandini and others, in folio in the Vatican Library—also an unpublished MS. in the Archives of the Vatican.

the winds and waves were stilled.* A circumstantial narrative of this occurrence exists in a manuscript in the Archives of the Vatican, and the histories of the Society refer to the fact. Still quoting from the letter in the Royal Library of Lisbon, we find that Silveira with five or six companions, all of whom were Portuguese, went to a village in the Quillamane district, where a Moorish king received them. From this place they sailed for the Zambesi, and when they entered that river conceived themselves in the great country of Monomotapa. Eight days afterwards they arrived at Inhanguona, whence they went to Sena, "which is a great centre of population, where abode then ten or fifteen Portuguese and some Indians already Christians." From this place Father Silveira paid a visit to the King of Inhamior, a vassal of Monomotapa, and went thence to Tete. We are told that he employed himself in prayer and evangelising the Portuguese, while, wherever possible,

* One writer thus describes what took place: "Father Silveira, in a great storm when about to perish, stretched out his arms and earnestly begged of God to still the tempest, which instantly subsided."

publicly teaching the Christian doctrine. An envoy was sent in front to the Emperor for permission to enter his great place or metropolis, and when this was obtained Father Silveira, putting up a bundle with chalice and sacred vessels, placed it on his shoulders and went forward on foot. He waded rivers, and when they were too deep was pushed across on a raft by Kafirs. At last, on Christmas Day, he entered Zimbaoe, where he was hospitably received by the Emperor, who himself came to meet him and sent presents of money, servants, and cows. At the same time he asked how much gold and land, and how many women he required. Silveira at once replied that he wanted none of these things, and the king remarked that "this man was not as others who come with much toil by sea and land to seek for treasures." Father Silveira had brought with him a statue of the Blessed Virgin, which he presented to the king, and it is asserted that this monarch for five nights consecutively saw in his dreams the Mother of God surrounded with great brilliancy. Father Silveira told the king that this was a divine language which nobody was able to understand unless he followed the law of the Creator of Heaven and Earth and the Redeemer of the human race. Two days afterwards the king and his mother desired to become Christians. After instructing them and a number of the courtiers in the commandments of God and the principal doctrines of the Christian religion, until he felt satisfied that they were adequately acquainted with them, he baptised them; the king taking the name of Sebastian and his mother that of Mary. One hundred oxen were sent on this occasion to Father Silveira, which he distributed among the poor.

The conversion of the Emperor and his courtiers to Christianity was looked upon with horror and dismay by the Mahometans at Zimbaoe, and everything in their power was done to poison the mind of the king against Silveira and Christianity.* Min-

* The authorities for Father Silveira's life are chiefly Letters from Fathers of the Society in the Collection in the Royal Library, Lisbon. Documents in the Archives and Library of the Vatican. The folio edition (Orlandini), "Historia Societatis Jesu." The "Life of Father Silveira," already quoted, published early in the seventeenth century. See also "L'histoire des choses plus

quame, a Moor from Mozambique, was the ringleader. They said that Silveira had come expressly from the Viceroy of India, and the authorities of Sofala not only tried to spy and reconnoitre, but even to induce the people to rebel against his Majesty. They added that Silveira was the most wicked and cunning enchanter in the whole world, and baptism was administered merely to place the baptised in his power. The prince was young, and his mother, "as is the custom of women," was nervous and suspicious, "therefore it was decided to take away the life of the body from him who had given them the life of the soul." Antonio Cuyada, who was present, tells us, "I know well," said Silveira, "that the king has determined to put me to death, but I am ready when it shall please God to give my life and my blood for His service." Cuyada laughed, and would not credit such a statement, but Silveira begged of him to get all the

memorables advenus tant ez Indes Orientales, que autres pays de la descouverts des Portugais," par le P. Pierre du Jarric Tolosain, de la meme Compagnie, S.J. Bordeaux Simon, Imprimeur, 1610. A process is about to be commenced in Rome for the beatification of Father Silveira, proto-martyr of South-eastern Africa.

Catholics to go to confession, and to receive Holy Communion, as he knew that his time was close at hand. He baptised about fifty persons, to whom he distributed some rosaries. Exhorting the Portuguese, he implored them to be always constant and firm in the faith and in the service of our Lord, notwithstanding the sufferings and persecutions which they would have to bear. So firm and tranquil was he that no one but Antonio Cuyada, to whom he had discovered it, knew that his death was close at hand. Shortly afterwards he ordered the sacred ornaments and vessels to be put in a place of safety. Meantime, the Portuguese having retired, Father Silveira remained by himself vested in the alb, holding the crucifix in his hand, and disposing himself for death, which he awaited hour after hour. Cuyada happening to return, Father Silveira said to him in a joyous tone, " I am more ready to receive death than my enemies are to give it to me. I pardon willingly the king and his mother, for they are seduced by the Mahometans."

The following is a narrative, by two servants who were present, of what occurred: " After

Antonio Cuyada had retired the Father commenced to walk before his lodgings, and that faster than customary. He sometimes raised his eyes to heaven, where he hoped shortly to see God, and he held the cross in his hands, offering his life for that Saviour who had given His life for him, and breathed forth heartfelt sighs. He subsequently retired to his chamber and prayed before the cross. Then he flung himself upon a bed of reeds and tranquilly slept. Eight soldiers who were watching flung themselves suddenly upon him and strangled him. One of them, called Macrumes, a barber with whom he used frequently to converse familiarly, dragged him from the bed. Thereupon he was taken by the feet and arms, raised up, and a cord placed round his neck, by means of which he was dragged backwards and forwards, during which time a great quantity of blood flowed from his mouth and nose.

"Thus was martyred Father Silveira on the 11th of August, 1561." The body was then dragged to the Mosengesses river, a tributary of the Zambesi, into which it was flung. "For these wretched Saracens had said that if a body of a man so wicked should remain on the earth it would infect the air, and would be the cause of a grievous pestilence."

A beautiful and romantic tradition exists regarding the remains of this martyr. Sixty years after his death a priest named Father Leo de Barbadas gives sworn testimony to the statement that when travelling to Mozambique he was cast by a storm on the coast at the mouth of the Zambesi river. Having come to a place where this great stream is divided into two parts, he found a dense wood, and saw a number of birds of exquisite beauty keeping guard on a great separated tree branch. Three Kafir youths who desired to penetrate into the forest were warned by fishermen against doing so in consequence of certain entrances being guarded by tigers. When Father Alphonsus asked the cause of this most extraordinary circumstance he was told that many years ago the corpse of a white man wearing a black tunic had arrived there fastened to a beam, and had by the force of the current been brought to a projecting bank, where it remained. Immediately tigers and a large number of other beasts seized the body and carried it inland, and from that time the birds began to rest on that branch. "The common opinion was that the man whose corpse was guarded must have been an excellent person, perhaps one of the minor gods." "Two youths reported that from the height of a tall tree they had seen the body of a priest guarded by tigers and other savage beasts, who kept watch around it." *

So soon as Father Silveira had been killed the king ordered that fifty Christians whom he had baptised should also be put to death. But a strange revulsion of opinion seems subsequently to have taken place. Many of the headmen and councillors were indignant at these atrocities, and said, with perfect justice, that if baptism were a capital offence the king himself ought to die. The Portuguese remonstrated against the iniquity of putting a person to death who only desired the salvation of others. Their indignation was naturally so great that not only did they threaten the Emperor with the anger of God Almighty, but

* We give the text of this curious tradition in the Appendix. The original was obtained in the Vatican Library.

pointedly referred to the necessity of taking up arms to punish the murderers of a man of noble blood. Like most savage potentates, the King of Monomotapa wished to keep on good terms with both sides, and lost no time in declaring that he had been seduced by evil men, and was exceedingly contrite. Two of the murderers of Father Silveira were killed by him, and the others escaped. It is added that Padre Antonio de Quadros, the Provincial of the society in India, who had sent Father Silveira to Monomotapa, as soon as he received news of his glorious martyrdom, desired to send other Fathers to carry on the work of the conversion of a nation watered by a martyr's blood. The Dominican order, however, had already been charged with the Portuguese missions in South-eastern Africa, and their missionaries succeeded those of the Society of Jesus.

The Portuguese felt the murder of Father Silveira not only to be a defeat but a gross insult to their flag, and knowing well that Monomotapa was worth fighting for, the circumstance was made a pretext for an invasion of the kingdom. In 1569 King

Sebastian sent a strong force of picked men, under the command of Francis Barreto, an experienced soldier, who had been governor of Portuguese India for many years. Father Monclaios, S.J., who was one of the chaplains of the expedition, has left us a narrative of events,* which we will follow. We are told that the king began this enterprise for three chief purposes. 1. To make the Gospel known. 2. To obtain riches from Monomotapa to support the great expenses of Portugal in India. 3. To take vengeance for the murder of Father Silveira. The ships arrived at Mozambique on May 16, 1570. "In all we were 700 men, of whom 550 soldiers were picked warriors." At this time the Governor of Sofala lived at Mozambique, and gold-dust was current money. A journey was taken to Quiloa, and here it is observed that "the Moorish population lie either in islands or very near the sea." Going *viâ* Zanzibar and Mombasa, they arrived at Melinde, and we are told that a very savage tribe of Kafirs named Mocequejos live in that country.

* In letters of the Jesuits from South-east Africa in folio volumes in the Royal Library of Lisbon.

"Starting from Melinde, we arrived at Cambo, a great and well-built city, whose queen was an extraordinarily faithful friend to the Portuguese. Our king has loaded her with presents, and Francis Barreto visited her in great state in the name of his Majesty." They then paid a visit to Pate, "where the most cruel enemies of the Portuguese live," thence to Zanzibar, and then back to Mozambique.

In November, 1572, we find the expedition of Barreto in twenty-two vessels on the river Zambesi, *en route* for the conquest of El Dorado. We are told that in this whole country there are no kings, but many "Fumos," who seem to be the lords of the land, some being strong and others comparatively weak. "All live in continual wars against each other." * Hippopotami and crocodiles abound in the rivers, and the latter animals are used by the Emperor of Monomotapa for the punishment of criminals, as men charged with crimes are thrown into the

---

* These letters contain long descriptions of the country and the people. The enormous number of hippopotami is referred to, and there is a dramatic description of a fight between a lion and a crocodile for a buffalo cow.

river, and if they swim across are considered innocent, whereas if devoured they are concluded to have been guilty and worthy of death. This system greatly curtailed the expenses of criminal administration.

When they arrived at Sena, the chief of that place visited Barreto, and they learned that the Emperor or high sovereign came here very often to taste the wine and to receive the stuffs with which the Portuguese desired to gratify his Majesty. Here also the Moors endeavoured to kill the Portuguese by means of poisoned meat.

Father Monclaios's references to the customs and manners of the barbarians, "as he saw them with his own eyes," deserve attention. He tells us that "the Fumos," or lower chiefs, frequently belong to the lowest class of men, are elected by their own countrymen, and frequently hold office against their will. Indeed, they sometimes desired Portuguese to accept these posts, and the explanation is to be found in the fact that officers of this rank were frequently required to give presents and "gratifications." "Above all Fumos is the Emperor of Monomotapa, a true king to whom obedience is truly paid, and whose eldest son is the heir. This Prince is very mighty, and reigns over vast regions and many vassals, among whom is the Fumo Panga, who can set in the field more than 70,000 soldiers. One of these tributaries is also the King of Batoa, in a country which we are told contains much gold. Another vassal is Lord of Manica, but he is not so rich. "When this country rests in peace our Portuguese go thither, either by way of Sofala or of Sena. . . . The Mongares are among the vassals of Monomotapa, and they pay him a tribute; and far inland many others, all in continual wars against each other without any controlling arm of justice. . . . They are very badly disposed to receive baptism and become Christians. . . . The gold mines lie near the capital of Monomotapa as well as in its provinces, and there are many of them. . . . The King had given some to the Portuguese, but as they were spending too much money to get gold in proportion to receipts, they abandoned the enterprise. Trading was more profitable. The negroes dig the ground and make galleries high and deep, the roofs of which from time to time fall upon their heads and kill them. When the king intends to get gold, he sends a cow to those who are digging. Each man is paid according to his work, but there are many tricks in vogue among the workers. The nature of the country opposes many difficulties to those who desire to conquer it. It is difficult for many soldiers to find subsistence, and little can be done except by way of trading, but in that very large profits are obtainable. Cotton trees grow well near Sena, and there cultivation on a large scale would prove successful."

In the vicinity of Sena, not far from the river, Gonçalo de Aranijo had discovered silver mines, and it is reported that they are very rich, and there are undoubtedly treasures of copper, iron, and tin, but the country itself is certainly an unhealthy one.

As the Moors had poisoned many men of the expedition, Barreto caused seventeen of their principal men to be put to death with torture, *pour encourager les autres*, while all their gold was seized and sent to the King of Portugal. An ambassador was then depatched with rich presents to the Emperor of Monomotapa, at his chief place Zimbaoe, distant 280 leagues from Sena, where the rich mines of Masapa are situated. This messenger announced that the Portuguese were in the country and that their Governor wished to treat of very important affairs, the settlement of which would confer great advantage upon the monarch and people of Monomotapa. They were sent by the very high and mighty Don Sebastian, King of Portugal and of the Indies, who desired peace and friendship—the large number of men in the Expedition being necessary for the purpose of opening up trade communications. The unfortunate ambassador was drowned in a river shortly after his arrival at Zimbaoe. As no reply arrived, Francis Barreto resolved in July, 1572, to break into the King's "possessions," going on along the river. Five companies of arquebusiers were formed, each one of which was two hundred strong, furnished with provisions and ammunition; behind was a corps of cavalry, and some cannons brought up the rear, while a fleet of twenty small vessels sailed up the Zambesi. "After getting over many difficulties by land and water, created by the perfidiousness of our enemies, by the poison of the natives, by the unwholesomeness of the climate, we arrived at Mongar a month after we had left Sena."

It was found absolutely necessary to subdue the fierce Mongares before any further progress could be made. They are described as robbers who continually made incursions into the neighbouring countries, and were dreaded by all the surrounding tribes. They had previously attacked the Portuguese at Tete and killed a number of them. Fortunately the King of Baroro, a chief named Chrombe, became an ally of Barreto, and furnished him with two hundred Kafirs to act as guides and bearers. A number of sick soldiers had to be left behind on an island, and then the expedition proceeded through narrow defiles until the army of the Mongares, twelve thousand strong, came in sight. The general skilfully disposed his forces, gave them battle, and put them utterly to rout, proving that the arrows and assegais of the savage men were poor weapons compared to those of the soldiers of civilisation. Of the Portuguese only two were killed and thirty wounded. Another battle had to be fought three days afterwards against even a greater army, when, it is said, no fewer than four thousand Kafirs were killed. Then the Mongares sued for peace, and sent Ambassadors to the camp. Barreto consented on condition that their plenipotentiaries should meet him at a place further in the interior, and declared that if this were not agreed to, he would desolate the country with fire and sword. This condition was accepted, and subsequently a treaty of peace was made at Musinda " as we were unable to overrun the country because of our sick and dead." The Mongares sent presents of cows, sheep, and gold. In describing the march to Musinda, the country is stated to be dreary and hilly, with occasionally a few badly cultivated fields. Other engagements with the natives took place, but the Kafir enemy was a trifling one compared to the insalubrity of the country. Disease increased among the members of the expedition " to extraordinary proportions," and "as many of ours died every day, it became impossible to go forward." Purchas in " His Pilgrimage " truly says " Francisco Barreto was discomfited not by the Negro, but by the Ayre, the malignity whereof is the same sauce of all their golden countries in Africa." There was no help for it. The powerful expedition which had gone forth with courage and enterprise was in such a crippled condition that its remnants had to go back again to the Portuguese possessions on the coast. However, there was a nominal acquisition of Monomotapa. An envoy was rather prematurely sent by the Emperor to Sena, followed by twelve personages, "one of whom was the King's Mayor and the other his son Moagem, Commander-in-chief of his army." The Monomotapa wished to be a friend of the King of Portugal, he was desirous of clearing the way of thorns, and should be happy to enter into a commercial treaty. Francis Barreto replied that the substantial points of any agreement must include the expulsion of Moors from the Empire, a donation of gold mines to Portugal, and the reception of missionaries with Christianity. He added that although at once obliged to go to Mozambique, he purposed to return and fully conquer all difficulties as he had done in the case of the Mongares.

The envoy in his reply stated that his people were delighted at the punishment that this nation of robbers had deservedly received, and added that the Emperor was himself about to send an expedition against them. It is observed by Father Monclaios that this was a correct statement, as subsequently a force from Monomotapa defeated the Mongares and ravaged a great part of their country.

Three Portuguese gentlemen, named Francis Megalhaes, Francis Refaxa, and Gaspar Borgis, were sent to Monomotapa with very rich and valuable presents, with which the Emperor was highly delighted, but the state of the unfortunate Portuguese expedition was most deplorable. There was absolute want of food, clothing, and medicines, deaths were numerous, and disease with famine walked hand in hand. They were in a malarial country which drew the energy and vitality from the soldiers, and the real reason of Barreto hastening to Mozambique was to endeavour to obtain supplies as quickly as possible. When Father Monclaios, as chaplain to Barreto, reached Quillamane with him he says, " The worst news waited for us." The greater part of their soldiers was dead, the rest were in a bad state, continually a prey to the most dangerous fevers. They were told that to go up the Zambesi to Sena would be merely to add to the number of the dead, but Barreto and the missionaries bravely answered that they were desirous of helping their brethren, and if necessary would die with them. After fifteen days' voyage Sena was reached, where they found only a miserable remnant of fifty soldiers. The captains of the four companies and all the other officers were dead, the surviving soldiers were so weak that they could scarcely stand, and the sick at the hospital all seemed to be rather dead than living men. Before such a scourge of mortality, the chronicler cries out, "Who could refrain from weeping? Of the eighty noblemen who had been set on shore in 1572 and taken part in the expedition there were only five living! And now the gallant and generous leader was to succumb. Eight days after landing he was attacked by the fever, and during his illness occupied himself with trying to encourage and cheer all those around him. Father Monclaios says, "He died a very good Christian, comforted with all the sacraments of the Church. He who had held in his hands such great riches did not leave after him even a penny to pay for his funeral." Thus passed away one of the greatest leaders the Portuguese in either India or Africa had ever known. He was experienced, brave, and capable. Immense pains and large expenditure supplied him with the best expedition Portugal could send out. He defeated warlike tribes, but all his seeming progress was merely like the wave breaking on a rock. Disease and pestilence prevented the possibility of substantial success and, the capture of Monomotapa by Portugal then, as at any other time, was merely nominal and illusory.

By order of King Sebastian, Don Vasco Fernandes was appointed the new governor. The ambassador from Monomotapa had arrived at Sena before even Barreto reached it, and his answer was that the Emperor was willing to expel the Moors from his kingdom, and indeed had already done so; that he was in no way responsible for the death of Father Silveira who had really been killed by the Moors; and that so far as the acceptance of

Christianity was concerned he was quite willing to consider the subject. The Emperor prayed the Portuguese to take possession of the gold and silver mines. The expedition, however, could not proceed to seize these sources of wealth. The Portuguese seemed, like Moses, to see the promised land and not to be able to enter it. A wretched remnant was left which had to hurry back to Mozambique. Father Monclaios says pointedly, "Others have written descriptions of the great quantities of gold and silver in the mines, but in the main all that we know is much less than is announced in Portugal. . . . They are digged out when people intend to buy stuffs for clothing; the King of Monomotapa had given such mines to some Portuguese who had gone to his court, but they soon abandoned them as the trade in stuffs and Indian mantles was far more important and profitable."

One of the greatest possible mistakes made by Portugal was that of sending an armed force under Barreto against the warlike natives of the interior. Her policy should rather have been by means of different methods to gain the affection and confidence of the people. Under any circumstances an error was committed when the enemy was undervalued, and an inadequate force sent against him—though it must be admitted that it was difficult to foresee the terrible disasters inflicted by the malarial climate. The littoral was an extremely extensive one, and to protect it alone was a work for which the strength of Portugal subsequently proved inadequate. So far as the interior is concerned there was, as we have said, never any real conquest of Monomotapa.

Not merely had the fierce natives of the interior to be encountered, but as early as the year 1586 the aggressions of the Turks became formidable. In the year just mentioned the Emir Ali Bey sailed from Mecca in two ships, and when he arrived on the South-eastern African coast, declared to the Arabs that his expedition was but the vanguard of a great fleet, and called upon them all to acknowledge the suzerainty of the Sultan of Constantinople. Many towns on the coast obeyed his orders, and several Portuguese were captured and sent into slavery. The Viceroy Don Duarte de Menezes was compelled to send out from Goa a fleet of eighteen vessels under the command of Martin Affonso de Melo Bombeyro, who burnt Mombasa, and reduced the other revolted towns to obedience. Again, in 1589, another fleet under Ali Bey attacked Melinda, but by means of a valiant resistance under Matheos Mendes de Vasconcellos the attack was repulsed. On this occasion the Governor in India had to send out a fleet of twenty vessels to protect the Portuguese possessions in South-eastern Africa. But the most ferocious and dangerous enemies of the Portuguese at this time were the Goths and Vandals of South Africa—the Zumbos—whose devastating hordes came from the north. They are described as a numerous Kafir tribe which descended on the littoral for the purposes of war and plunder. The unfortunate Moors were attacked by them at this time, and were consequently in the dreadful position of being driven by barbarians from the interior on to the swords of the Portuguese who attacked them by sea. Advancing to Quiloa the Zumbos themselves threatened that town, and by means of the treachery of a Mahometan were led by a secret way into the fortress and massacred the inhabitants. Diego de Couto informs us that three thousand prisoners were devoured by their cannibal assailants. Subsequently these fierce savages spread along the coast and massacred a large number of Moors. Their progress, however, at last was checked by the Portuguese at Melinde.

Captain Lancaster * tells us that in 1591 when he visited Zanzibar he found the position of the Portuguese then very precarious, and Guillain † says that in Mozambique, Sena, and Tete, which were their principal dependencies, they were constantly in contact with warlike people. The latter author refers to Tete as a Portuguese fortress built on the right bank of the Zambesi, around which there were about eleven villages inhabited by Kafirs who were ruled locally by *encosses*, all under the sovereign authority of the Captain of Tete, who had the power of appointing and deposing

---

* See Captain James Lancaster's voyage in " Histoire Générale des Voyages," tome i. book ii. chap. xvi.

† Guillain, "Documents sur l'Afrique Orientale," tome i. p. 405.

them. Troublesome people they must have been, as "they rather prefer to fight, say they, than to till the ground. The warrior who dies fighting needs to work no more, whilst he who survives is rich in the spoil of his enemies." The two peoples near Tete who were not vassals are described as the Zimbas or Mouzimbas and the Moumbos—all were cannibals, and Diego de Couto adds, "sellers of man's flesh in shops or booths." One tribe was constantly asking for assistance against another. At one time we find Fernandes de Chaves successful by means of fighting with the assistance of the Moumbos, on another occasion the Captain of Sena, Andre de Santiago, was disastrously unsuccessful. This unfortunate soldier was surprised by the Ouazimba before he could effect a junction with troops from Tete, and as a consequence Sena fell into the hands of the savages, and "three hundred Portuguese were all killed and devoured by these cannibals." Don Pedro de Souza had to come to the relief from Mozambique, and with two hundred Portuguese and five hundred Kafirs crossed the Zambesi and besieged a fortified camp of the enemy. Soon, however, the merchants and cultivators who formed a large part of the Europeans decided to retire, and the whole force was obliged to retreat with considerable loss. Shortly afterwards the Ouazimba sent a message in which, while justifying their hostilities, they expressed a desire to live henceforward on good terms with the Portuguese, and therefore proposed peace. Of course Don Pedro de Souza accepted the offer with the utmost alacrity.

The Portuguese were successful at Mombasa, and the Viceroy Albuquerque erected a fortress there in 1594, but a new enemy was now about to come into the field. Two Dutch ships anchored near Mozambique in 1597 and afterwards seized some Portuguese vessels; but the first hostilities of any consequence began in 1607 when Admiral Van Coerden, with a fleet of eight ships, endeavoured in vain to capture Mozambique. After an interval of six months Van Coerden returned, but had again to abandon the enterprise. At this time the seat of Portuguese government in South-east Africa, hitherto fixed at Sofala, was changed to Mozambique. In July, 1608, Admiral Verhoeven appeared with a fleet of thirteen vessels against this port, disembarked his troops, and commenced a regular siege, but experienced such an heroic resistance that he was at last compelled to retire, not, however, before he shot all his Portuguese prisoners in revenge for a deserter from his side not having been delivered up. In 1609 some of the men of the English frigate *Union* were killed by Portuguese in an ambuscade at Zanzibar. However, the time had not yet come for Great Britain to assert herself in the East, and the Arabs of the coast as well as the fierce Kafirs of the interior were at that time the only serious obstacles to Portuguese rule.

Guillain says that " Pride and cupidity, theft and violence : these four words seem to sum up Portuguese domination. Mombasa, more than any other locality, was a proof of it. It appeared destined, says Faria y Souza, to have for commandants of its fortress, officers who were most insolent and avaricious. . . . Wisdom and prudence were words devoid of sense for men whom the love of gain devoured, and who, thinking more of their own private interests than those of the country, remained inaccessible to sentiments of justice and of gratitude. . . . In 1614 the fortress of Mombasa had for its captain a man who was even more insolent and greedy than any of his predecessors, named Manoel de Melo Pereira," who seized a pretext to occupy the Moorish town. Ahmed, the Mahometan Sheik, took refuge among the Kafirs who urged him to make war upon the Portuguese, which he refused to do. Without his assistance however they attacked the Europeans and were defeated. Subsequently the unfortunate Ahmed was seized and assassinated.

In Monomotapa " the Emperor " triumphed over the King of Monga by means of assistance rendered to him by the Portuguese, and in order to show his gratitude, he made a perpetual donation " of all the mines " of his country to the King of Portugal. This offer was accepted on the 1st of August, 1607, by Diogo Simoens Madeira. In substance the deed of gift ran as follows : " That the Emperor gave all the mines of gold, of silver, of copper, of tin, of iron, and of lead, which should be found in his empire to the King of Portugal, on condition that this Prince should aid him with his military forces, and recognise him as his brother in arms; that the year following he would send one of his sons to Goa; that he placed at once in the hands of Don Diogo Simoens two other sons, and that he would soon confide to them two of his daughters in order that they might be made Christians." Shortly afterwards one of the vassals of Monomotapa rebelled, the Portuguese soldiers under Simoens Madeira went to the rescue, and victory resulted. The two young princes, as they are styled, became Christians under the names of Philip and of Diogo; one remained at Tete, and the other returned to his parents. "The Emperor" unfortunately trusted too much to his previous success, and endeavouring with his own forces to defeat malcontents at Baroe, suffered a defeat there. One of his enemies named Matouziaque took advantage of the opportunity to make himself master of a large portion of Monomotapa; but the Portuguese allies being called upon to help, Nuno Alvarez Pereira, Captain-General of Mozambique, came to the rescue, and Simoens Madeira, with a force to assist the Emperor, who was re-established in his possessions after two signal victories had been gained over his enemies by the Portuguese. These occurrences took place in 1609. Estevam d'Ataide, who succeeded Pereira as Captain-General, saw that it was evidently the interest of Portugal to do everything possible to secure the rich gold mines, and as a means to that end sent out expeditions against the enemies of Monomotapa, and constructed a fort in the district of Mosapa, which he garrisoned with an adequate force under the command of Diogo do Carvalho, who had frequently to sally forth in order to check the incursions of marauders.

The yield of the mines of Monomotapa was at this time (1609) said to be considerable, and it was the custom, whenever a new Captain-General was appointed, to send a present valued at five thousand ducats to the Emperor. When Estevam d'Ataide assumed office he sent the commandant of the fort at Mosapa on a mission respecting the mines, but purposely omitted to send the usual present. This was a fatal mistake. At first there was silence, and then indignation. Why should the Portuguese go on helping themselves to gold without fulfilling one of the principal conditions which entitled them to it? Merchandise was seized, and Carvalho became so enraged that he headed a secret party which surprised the people of Monomotapa, and put many of them to death; subsequently he abandoned his fort and returned to Tete. Estevam d'Ataide then repaired to Sena, and declared that he was now obliged, with regret, to take forcible possession of the mines; however, learning that the Dutch were attacking Mozambique, he hastened to the coast leaving Diogo Simoens Madeira, captain at Tete, in command. The war went on, and the Emperor sent envoys to ask for peace, but haughty D'Ataide would not even see them. A long and expensive war was the result, and the Viceroy of Goa evidently became dissatisfied, as in the year 1613 the Governor of Mozambique was recalled and Dom Joao Azevedo appointed in his stead.

The mines can scarcely have been valued very highly, as at this time we find Diogo Simoens Madeira carrying on a war against the Emperor of Monomotapa with only one hundred and forty Portuguese soldiers at his disposal. His auxiliaries, however, comprised six thousand Kafirs. He was very successful against the chief Chomba. Then he directed his march to the district of Chichova where mines of silver existed. The astute Emperor endeavoured to check hostilities by offering these mines to the Portuguese. Simoens Madeira rose to the bait and offered to give stuffs of the value of four thousand ducats for these valuable acquisitions, but just before their surrender the Emperor found some pretext for delay; a quarrel ensued, and war broke out on a larger scale and with greater intensity. In March, 1615, an army of ten thousand Kafirs attacked a fort garrisoned by forty Portuguese, but Simoens Madeira came to the rescue and gained a complete victory. Unfortunately, these successes became illusory in consequence of terrible sickness and mortality among the troops. The climate was more disastrous than the enemy. Simoens Madeira appealed to the Viceroy at Goa for assistance, and informed him that without help the great successes just obtained would be in vain. Reinforcements were sent, but they were detained at Mozambique by Fonseca Pinto who was Governor. He pretended to doubt the actual existence of the gold mines, and made this a pretext for the gratification of feelings of jealousy and hatred entertained towards Simoens Madeira. Three months were lost, and then a despatch was received which made the Governor of Mozambique responsible for the loss of the conquest. The reply was a brutal order of confiscation against all the goods of the officer who had dared to send such a letter and a traitorous message to Monomotapa informing the Emperor that Simoens Madeira was a mere bandit endeavouring to seize the gold mines without any authorisation from the Viceroy. Subsequently an infamous order was sent from Mozambique to waylay and kill one of the most able and successful officers who ever fought for Portugal in South-eastern Africa. Simoens Madeira, hearing of his peril, abandoned the fort of Chicova, and for doing so was at once declared a rebel and had to fly to Tete. "So terminated the second conquest of the mines of Monomotapa," says Guillain; "the first caused the death of Barreto, the latter seized from Simoens Madeira all that which makes a man wish not to die, honour, consideration, riches."

What has now been told can be read in the pages of the Portuguese historian Faria, and the details unfortunately show a sad system of maladministration and degradation of character. There was constant trouble on the entire South-east African littoral. Abbas Shah of Persia entered into an alliance with Great Britain, and in 1620 the fort of Queixoma (Kechm) was attacked. Hormous subsequently was seized, and this was a triumph which entailed most serious consequences, as it immensely increased the Arab influence and power on the entire coast. At Mombasa disastrous results ensued from making a *protégé* of the son of Sultan Ahmed. This youth, who was baptised in 1627 under the name of Dom Geronimo Chingaulia, pretended for many years to renounce the Mahometan religion, but at last being suspected by the Portuguese, turned upon them with fury and massacred men, women, priests, religions, and infants. Francisco de Moura was sent out against him from Goa in 1631, and was eventually able with eight hundred marines and soldiers to attack Mombasa. A long and unsuccessful siege ensued. However, a blockade followed, and the Sultan, believing that discretion was the better part of valour, fled to Arabia with all the riches he was able to carry away, while the abandoned island which had assumed a desert appearance was easily retaken by the Portuguese. An inscription at Mombasa informs us that in 1635, Captain Major Francisco de Sexas e Cabra relieved the fortress, reduced the coast of Melinda, and rendered certain sheiks tributary.

It must be borne in mind that the Portuguese, when substituting their authority for that of the Moors, did not entirely dispossess them of authority and were content that they should be in the position of suzerains and vassals, the latter paying an annual tribute. The sheiks saw the impossibility of armed resistance, and agreed to this arrangement. The Portuguese learned the character of the Arab trade and, obtaining goods from India, carried on commerce advantageously.

As we have seen, Sofala was at one time the seat of government, and subsequently Mozambique, but all settlements were ruled from Goa, the residence of the Viceroy. On the Southeast African coast there were two circumscriptions, the first of which included * the districts of Sofala, of Mozambique, and of the establishments on the Zambesi (Osrios de Cuama), while the second included the coast from Cape Delgado to Cape Guardafui, the chief seaport being Mombasa. The Portuguese were not able to hold the latter, and before the close of the seventeenth century the Arabs of Oman ruled this country. The

* From "The Oriente conquestado," cong. v., d. 11, p. 853, we learn that the kingdoms comprised between the countries of Inhambane and the division of Louabo were the following: to the north of Inhambane the kingdom of *Chicangam*, having for northern limit the river *Sabia*; then the kingdom of *Sedenda*, which stretches to the lands of Sofala; here commences the kingdom of Quiteve, terminating at a river which the Portuguese name *Tendanculo*; the territory comprised between this and the right bank of the Zambesi was regarded as a Portuguese possession. All these kingdoms formed part of the empire of Monomotapa.

"Bankers' Geography," quoted by Batelho, states that Monomotapa is an extensive country bounded on the east by the kingdom of Sofala, on the west by the mountains of Kaffrarla, on the north by the river Cuama, which separates it from Monoemugi, and on the south by the history of the wars which raged there is very obscure, and there is even great divergence of opinion respecting the date of the capture of Mombasa. Our business of course is merely to refer to the principal events which marked Portuguese rule generally in South-east Africa, adverting more particularly to occurrences in Sofala and Monomotapa.

The heroic period of Portuguese colonial history commences with Prince Henry the Navigator and terminates early in the seventeenth century. This was the grand epoch

river Espirito Santo. It is situated between 41° and 56° E. long., and 14° to 25° S. lat., having 960 miles of length from east to west, and 660 miles of breadth from north to south.

This country is divided into six provinces or petty kingdoms, which are vassals of Monomotapa properly so called, viz., Quetive, Manica, Inhambane, Inhamur, and Sabia, or Save. Camoens, in the "Lusiad," says (Chant x., stance 93):

"Ve do Benemotapa, O grande Imperio
De salvatica gente, negra e nua;
Onde Goncalo morte e vituperio
Padacera pela Fe sancta sua,
Nasce por este incognito hemispherio
O metal, perque mais a gente sua:
Vê que do lago, d'onde se derrama
O Nilo, tambem vindo esta Cuama."

which produced great kings, illustrious statesmen, intrepid mariners, and most devoted missionaries, but it cannot be denied that there was a great decadence subsequently. We agree with Guillain in thinking that the accession of a strange dynasty to the throne of Emmanuel contributed much to disturb the empire which that great king had founded beyond the seas, and indeed probably hastened its ruin. When John IV., Duke of Braganza, in 1640 re-established the kingdom of Portugal, it was then almost too late to change the fate of distant Portuguese possessions. England and Holland had already made large breaches in those of India, and the wars which the home country was compelled to carry on in Europe prevented the possibility of adequate forces being sent to the extremities of the empire.

We have now really finished all important Portuguese history affecting Monomotapa. The country was never really conquered. The mines were acquired by a deed of gift or of cession, but this right eventually lapsed, and the power of Portugal from various reasons dwindled in South-eastern Africa until it could with difficulty repress native incursions and retain a few forts on the Zambesi, besides various seaports along the coast. It would be tiresome, as well as useless and uninteresting, to enter into details of numerous conflicts and miserable quarrels. Decadence continued, and in the eighteenth century the superior attractions of Brazil eclipsed altogether the reputation of Ophir. The true position of Monomotapa we desire to describe in the words of their own writers. The author of an able essay on "Les Champs d'Or," submitted in 1891 to the Royal Geographical Society of Lisbon, tells us that, "Opposite Tete commenced Mokaranga, or Monomotapa properly so called, whose dominion was reserved to its sovereign with a species of authority over the kingdoms of Barnue and of Manica. In Mokaranga, which embraced a space of 150 leagues more or less, the Portuguese had also their captains at Dambarare, Angoe, Luari, and Chipuravuri, subordinated to a Captain-General who resided at Zimbaoe, at the Court of Monomotapa. There was always a captain at Manica. Gold attracted traffickers, who travelled through those lands which were covered with Portuguese fairs. The first was that of Luanze, four days south of Tete." Then there were the fairs of Bocoto Massapa, and more south those of Massaqueca and Bandire. "The kingdom of Manica was one entire mine of gold."* Father Manoel Barreto says, "All Mokaranga is a perpetual mine of gold. . . . Frere Antonio da Conceicao describes a fair in a most remote district, and in fact there were no doubt numerous ports and fairs throughout these territories." As the writer just quoted says: "The age of gold for us was when we were in contact with the indigenous chiefs." This time was allowed to pass by, and the success which possibly might have been retained by means of good policy passed away with it. In 1693 the Portuguese were attacked by Chengamira, a vassal of the Emperor of Monomotapa, were easily surprised,

* Manoel Barreto has left us interesting information about working the gold. He says that the gold from the rivers was preferred to that from the mines. Pits were made and at certain times a ladder was let down and the Kafirs extracted "quartz gold"; when an irruption of water took place work was suspended. The Portuguese alone knew the secret of gold here and kept it to themselves. Certainly the Dutch at the Cape seemed to be in complete ignorance of it, although most desirous to discover El Dorados, and frequently sending out expeditions in search of them.

and a number of the inhabitants of Sena and Tete were slain. The Portuguese force had to retire from Zimbaoe, a great war ensued, and help from Goa was invoked. Dom Estevao da Gama penetrated into the Zambesi country, but died at Sena, and Chengamira, profiting from this circumstance, entered Manica and completely destroyed the fair of Massaqueca. "The power which we had exercised in these regions became sensibly enfeebled," says a Portuguese writer.* In 1769, 'the Captain-General Pereira do Lago endeavoured to restore the fair of Dambarare, "but the time of fairs was passed." This writer also gives us the reason for the decadence of the power of his country in South-eastern Africa, attributing it in part to the capture of Bacaim by the Mahrattas in 1739 and to the great attraction of the Brazil diamond mines.

It is desirable to review the records of missionary enterprise in Monomotapa and the countries immediately connected with it, so as to obtain additional information.† We

* "Les Champs d'Or," previously quoted, p. 26.

† The information respecting Dominican Missions is chiefly obtained from the great work in folio contained

have seen that the Jesuits formed the vanguard. Shortly after the martyrdom of Father Silveira that Order gave way to the Dominican, which had in a general Chapter in the year 1546 accepted the charge of South-eastern Africa, and deputed its management to the Portuguese province. In 1577 priests of this Order were sent to Mozambique, who founded there the Church and Monastery of the Holy Rosary, while at the same time other missionaries were despatched to the interior. The Sofala Mission was founded in 1586, and at a very early date that of St. Katharine of Sienna was established at Sena on the Zambesi. Tete and others followed. The shipwrecks, labours, and martyrdom of Father Nicolao do Rosorio

in the house of the Father-General of the Dominicans at Rome, entitled "Da Historia de St. Domingo Particular Do Reino e Conquistas de Portugal," por Father Luis Concega. In the library at this house there is an excellent engraving of the seventeenth century, representing the baptism of an Emperor of Monomotapa in 1652. In Latin we are told that he was baptised "after having been devoutly instructed in the faith Apostolic and Catholic Roman by the Fathers of St. Dominick." The ceremony took place on August 4, 1652. The Emperor was named Dominick, and his wife Louise. Numerous other expected conversions are referred to.

form the most interesting events chronicled. This missionary sailed from Portugal, and when "he arrived at the Cape of Good Hope was assailed with the usual tempests," and subsequently was wrecked at "the Land of Smoke" (Natal), which is described as a part of Southern Ethiopia. Two of his companions were sent into the country, where they found a village of Kafirs who gave them food, and behaved so well towards them that "they believed they could have remained for ever among those barbarians." At last, after many difficulties, they arrived at Sofala, where they found a House of St. Dominick and brothers under Father Joao Santos, a superior who afterwards wrote the famous History of Ethiopia. Father Nicolao went thence to Mozambique, and, although he had the option of going to Goa or returning to Portugal, "offered himself for fevers and suffering by consenting to go to Cuama and Kaffraria, where he will die."

Father Nicolao had been residing at Tete for some time when he received the appointment of Chaplain to Andre de Santiago, Captain of Sena, who "was determined to fight the barbarians in order to destroy them before they grew in power." These savages are thus described: "The Zimbas or Muzimbas are new people who from their native parts have entered Ethiopia, killing everything. They are 20,000 in number, without any women, wives, or sons, kill and devour everything, eating human flesh. They are to this country what the Goths, Huns, and Vandals were to Europe. They advanced quickly through many lands, and, as they met with no resistance, desolated all. The natives hide their provisions and join these barbarians to escape death and their teeth. They ran through three hundred leagues on the shores and entered Monomotapa, entrenched themselves, and went out on excursions. The Portuguese fortified themselves on the Zambesi at places distant sixty leagues one from the other—one of these being Sena and the other Tete—both under the orders of the Captain-General of Sofala. These places serve as factories in order to collect gold." Santiago was more brave than discreet, as he committed the terrible and common mistake of underrating the enemy, who by means of spies had learnt full particulars respecting both his intentions and preparations. A squadron of picked savage warriors was sent out at night, which suddenly fell upon the Portuguese when marching without any order or precaution, and as a consequence there was no fighting, but merely indiscriminate slaughter. " The barbarians fell upon the Portuguese before they could get ready, and they were all killed, and no one escaped." Father Nicolao, although mortally wounded, was found living by the Kafirs, who tied his hands together, brought him to a village, and then, fastening him to a tree, finished his martyrdom—" killing him because of their hate of the Christian religion." He received his death with fortitude and joy, not inaptly being compared to St. Sebastian. We are told that " the barbarians then went into the island of Quiloa, where they ate many Arabs," subsequently killed every one at Mombasa, but were eventually defeated by the King at Melinde, who fought against them with other Kafirs, people of valour. " So the Lord God destroyed an instrument with which he had punished others." In connection with this subject we are told that " another army of barbarians like this was many years ago running through the same coast of Eastern Ethiopia, because the coast extends to the Cape of Good Hope. They are called Jagas, and now they are going into the kingdom of Angoa. They are scourges of God."

The South-eastern African province of the Dominicans was in 1579 styled " The province of the Rosary," and Father Antonio de Souza was Provincial. The Viceroy Albuquerque assigned them 100,000 reis as yearly income, and by degrees their missionaries spread up the Zambesi and into Monomotapa. " In every such land were many Portuguese whom the thirst of gold had thrown there. Avarice is a species of idolatry." A very bad account is given of the Europeans, who are described as having " already lost the knowledge of Christians and thrown away the obligations of Faith—the commandments of God and of the Church. They did not observe either Sundays or Festivals, and made no distinction of days in Lent and Fridays. . . . The Fathers did their best with prayers, corrections, and admonitions, gaining many souls to Christ."

In 1733 a missionary named Father Antonio dos Prosaies writes that in Monomotapa there is a "vast congregation and many churches." An Emperor had been baptised by the Dominicans in 1652, and this conversion became the subject of great congratulation, but so unsettled did the country become that the advantages anticipated did not result. Nevertheless, Christian missions continued fairly successful considering the awful position of the continent subject to the incursion of great bands of marauding savages.

But to carry them on with permanent success it was essential that Portugal should be able really to master Monomotapa and the interior. This she was not able to do. Her power began to wane after the middle of the seventeenth century, and Christianity suffered. The missionaries lost prestige with protection. Civilisation was unable to stem the tide of savagery, and the Portuguese had eventually to be contented with a strip of coast and a few small towns on the Zambesi. The Dominican order itself greatly diminished in number and power during the eighteenth century, and it must be remembered that only Portuguese members of it could be sent to Portuguese possessions. We find them struggling on until in the nineteenth century they had churches and missionaries only in the most important places. In 1818 Father de Santa Maria was appointed Superior at Mozambique, and even in 1826 there is reference to a successor, but certainly before the year 1830 the last Dominican had left the shores of Portuguese Southern Africa.

Portuguese writers of the present day complain with justice of the manner in which the great services of their nation in the cause of African discovery and geography are ignored. In illustration of what has been done by Portugal for African geography and to show what was known in the sixteenth century concerning it, we subjoin a synopsis of facts and arguments taken from an able work placed at our disposal, entitled "L'Hydrographie Africaine au XVI. Siècle d'après les premiers explorations Portuguese," par M. Luciano Cordeira. King John II. of Portugal was the true initiator of geographical explorations in Africa. The Empire of Prester John was specially sought after by him. The idea of a great central lake where the Zaire or Congo took its source existed first in Portugal. Barros says distinctly that King John desired Ruy de Sousa at the Congo to pursue the course of the river to its source in "the Great Lake." Upon the very early German map published by the Marquis of Lavradie in 1867, and attributed to the year 1489, there occur the words, "Hic est vera forma moderna affrice secundum descriptione Portugalensium." In one of the maps of the Portuguese Atlas of Lazaro Luis, published in 1563, we see a great lake placed above the kingdom of Quiloa, and from this the Zambesi flows. A beautiful map of the world of Fernas Vaz Dourado, published in 1571, is of the same character. There is a great central lake situated between 10° and 12° S. latitude, from which flows the Zambesi and the Counza to the south, the Nile to the north, and the Zaire or Congo, detaching itself, proceeds in a westerly direction. In the work of Pigafetta there is a good map of Africa by Duarte Lopez, published in 1591, on which is incribed "L'Africa e il Capo de Buonna Speranza e il laghi del Nilo e il monte donde scende e il Reami de Prete Janni e di Congo e le contrade uicine." The geography of De Barros is unfortunately lost, but this author says in his "Asia" that "all the country which we have designated the kingdom of Sofala is a great land governed by an idolatrous prince named Bonomotapa. This is girdled like an island by two arms of a river which flows from the greatest lake in all Africa—a lake which ancient authors desired much to know, because it was the mysterious source of the celebrated Nile, from which also flows the Zaire through the kingdom of Congo." We find an old Portuguese explorer (Castanhoso) telling us that Prester John of Abyssinia had savage Kafirs in the interior who carried a great quantity of gold to his fairs in small sacks. Lopes very exactly says, "Besides the three kingdoms above mentioned—Quiloa, Melinde, and Mombasa—the great kingdom of Monemugi extends westerly towards the interior, which is bounded on the south by the kingdom of Mozambique and the Empire of Monomotapa, by the River Coava, and towards the east (Lualaba Nil) with the Nile, between the two lakes, and has for its limits on the north the empire of Prester John." Santos declares that the Nile flows from a great lake named Barzona. Sir Lucius Cordeira sums up by saying that the general ideas of Portuguese geography of the sixteenth century comprised the knowledge—(1) Of a central and lake origin of the Zaire, Zambesi, and Nile. (2) Correction of ptolemaic geography by the affirmation of the existence of two great lakes besides others. (3) Prolongment towards the equator towards the South of the Zaire. (4) Determinate approximation of the position of the basin of the Nile.*

* The map of Africa as known to the world in the middle of the seventeenth century, published in this book, is the best of many found in the Archives of the Vatican. The author has searched for maps of Africa not only in Rome, both at the Vatican and Propaganda, but in the library of St. Mark's at Venice, and in the great Bibliothèque Nationale, Paris. The very early maps are disappointing, but those based upon the narratives of missionaries, &c., published early in the seventeenth century, of which we furnish a specimen in this volume, are well filled up, and comprise interesting and valuable information. The map in the Propaganda sent to the Chicago Exhibition has been copied for this book, but it is of such a mere outline character that we do not publish it.

We have a sincere desire to do justice to the Portuguese, and have been guided in our narrative of events by their own writers. When we arrive at the present century we find this people only holding on to the skirt of South-eastern Africa. Their missions, fairs, and trade had dwindled until the shadow of the prosperity of former times merely lingered. The gold mines were more a tradition than a reality, the last Dominican missionary left before the year 1830, and trifling native disputes with the sluggish trivial trade of a neglected colony alone remained. When Delagoa Bay was claimed by the British Empire the decaying flame of ambition and rivalry flickered for a time. The question was not then a very important one and was submitted to the arbitration of Marshal M'Mahon. The President of the French Republic decided in favour of the claims of Portugal, and recent events have induced a weak and waning nation to cling to this gateway, to one of the El Dorados of the world, with the tenacity and persistency of those who wish to retain some portion at least, not merely of the glories, but of the acquisitions of their ancestors.

It has been thought wise to conclude this work at a period previous to the conquest of Monomotapa by the British South Africa Company. Certainly it seems almost incongruous to enter into a great arena of present-day controversy in a book whose principal object is to consider the problems of remote antiquity, and this modern history is treated of in another work by the present writer.

APPENDICES.

APPENDIX A.

COMPLETE LIST OF DOCUMENTS IN THE ARCHIVES OF THE VATICAN CONCERNING AFRICA, WITH LIBRARY REFERENCE SO AS TO ENABLE STUDENTS TO OBTAIN THEM.

1. 1282. Petras tragoniæ Rex prætexta procedendi in Africam, insulam Siciliæ invadit. Ber. ep. 502, 513.
2. 1283. Vandalinæ regnum (fortasse in Africa) a Regi Castillæ possessum pacifice. Ber. ep. 492.
3. Robertus Episcopus Morocho Legatus in Africam. Nicol. 4, 11, 844, 855.
4. 1436. Africæ terrarum conquestam ait ad se spectare Rex Castellæ. Martin. V., 12, p. 157.
5. 1344. Insulæ Africæ concessæ Ludovico de Hispania. Bullas. 62, p. 61.
6. 1442. Cruciata pro Alfonso Rege Portugalliæ contra Saracenos Africæ abeque tamen procindicio Joannis Regis Castillæ quoad conquestam castrorum ete; indultum. Eng. 4, to. 1, pp. 216, 219.
7. Indulgentia ad decretam affectam, p. 221. Recipitur sub stylica protectione civitas. Ceutæ in Africa, 222.
8. 1514. De expeditione Africana Ferdinandi Aragonum et Siciliæ Regis. Brev. Minut., to. 2, No. 550.

APPENDIX A.

9. 1526. De tramitibus Portugalliæ Regi pro fidei manu tentione. Arm. XI., caps. 1, No. 175.
   Petri Rubei discursus ad Gregoriam XIII. de bello Africæ.
10. Arm. X., caps. 6, No. 55.
    Gregorii 13 bulla conciatæ pro Redemptione captivorum.
13. Africæ in bello in quo occubuit Sebastionus Portugalliæ. Rex. Arm. g. caps. 4, No. 6.
14. Hieronyimo Tangorin Mombasæ et Melindi Regi in Africa. Urb. 8, an. 10, p. 6.
15. Epistola Regi Africæ ex Massilia, 16 Aug., 1548.
16. Descriptio civitatis Ceutæ in Africa Portogallo, to. 2, p. 404.
17. Descriptio Civitatis Oran in Africa Port. To. 2, p. 406.
18. Sermo coram Rege Catholico cupiente exercitum in Africam ducere. Politicor. to. 79, p. 365.
19. Sebastianus Portugalliæ Rex petit auxilium a Pontifice pro eundo in Africam. 64, to. 30, pp. 346, 350.
20. Quare idem Rex in Africam contendit, Aug., 1578. Politicor. to. 17, to. 18, pp. 89–97. Pio 77, p. 29.
21. Negotium Africæ fovetur = Aless. 4, 1. 691. Dispensatio matrimonii pro Christianis Africæ, 4, IV., 311.
22. De expeditione contra Saracenos Africæ. Ebolo 2476. Tragoniæ Regis transfretare debent in Africa contra Saracenos. Ebolo 3041, 3042.
23. Antonii de Sousa super modo javandi Religionem Catholicam et Captivos apud Infideles Africæ. Arm. caps. 4, No. 6.

24. 1244, 23 Mart. De Decima pro subsidio terræ Sanctæ in Regnis Castellæ et Legionis concessi Regi ob defensionem corundam adversus Saracenos Africæ.
Nicolaus III. concessit Decimus Regi Castellæ contra Saracenos. Ber. ep. 482.
25. Maratur Martinus 4 quod Rex Aragoniæ Africam tot manitionibus divitiis et populis refertam, inconsulta Sede Apostolia invadere tentaverit. Ber. ep. 486.
26. Philippo de Africa Principi Monarchi. Clem. g. an. 1, p. 46.

APPENDIX B.

COPIES OF ALL DOCUMENTS IN THE ARCHIVES OF THE PRO-
PAGANDA AT ROME RESPECTING MONOMOTAPA AND
ADJACENT COUNTRIES (TRANSLATED), OBTAINED UNDER
ORDER OF HIS EMINENCE CARDINAL LEDOCHOWSKI,
PREFECT OF " PROPAGANDA."

In 1630 the Holy See, having learned that the Emperor of Monomotapa had been converted by Fr. Louis of the Holy Ghost, a Dominican, made inquiries about it from the Sacred Congregation of Missionaries. They wrote to Portugal, and in 1632 ten missionaries, by order of His Most Faithful Majesty, set out for Monomotapa. After that time, says Cerri, we have had no further news.

Original MSS. (Portugal) 1630, v. 98, p. 35. Lorenzo, Bishop of Gerace, Colletore of Portugal, writes to the Propaganda :—

LISBON, *Oct.* 12, 1630.

That which has been done in the kingdom of Monomotapa by Bro. Louis of the Holy Ghost in propagation of our Holy Faith, Your Eminence will see in the letter which he has written to his Provincial translated from Portuguese into Italian.

Copy of the Letter from Fr. Louis, from Goa, to the Provincial at Portugal.

Feb. 3, 1630.

In the year 1628, on the 17th of November, the Emperor of Monomotapa was stirred up against the Christians and killed the ambassador whom the Captain of Mozambique had sent to his court, as well as all the other Christians who were in his country. All the men of that place took advantage of my being in Tete as vicar, and requested me to come to Sena as their representative, in order to bring them succour by which they might at least save life and goods. I accepted this labour for the love of our Lord and honour of religion. I came to Sena and obtained from the captain and inhabitants of the said place the required assistance, and started with them for Alvaure, which is the first station, and not finding the enemy there, we went to Mocapa, where we found the army of the Emperor, which consisted of a hundred thousand men, and ours not more than fifteen thousand.

With this inequality, invoking the help of God through the intercession of our Lady of the Rosary, our little army attacked this great one, and by the help of God put them to flight. Having obtained this victory we went with our army to Zimbabwe, the court of the King, and there I built a little church and put up a crucifix I had brought with me, and a statue of the Blessed Virgin of the Rosary, dedicating the Church to her and calling it "of the Rosary." I said a Mass *in gratiarum actionem* for the help bestowed. I put an uncle of the conquered king, called Manura, in possession of the kingdom, he being the eldest of the other brothers. I made him tributary to the Catholic King, with the conditions which your Reverence will find herewith. In this likewise I had much trouble, for the Portuguese wished to put another relative of the conquered king in possession who had brought them to Sena with great promises of gain. However, as God favours truth and justice, I obtained that which I claimed. The King being in authority, I sought to convert him to our Holy Faith. When I had spent eight months in this daily work, it pleased God to move the heart of the King so that he received the waters of Holy Baptism. I administered it to him, and as *Regis ad exemplum totus componitur orbis*, the great people of the country began to be converted, and four or five of them were baptised with the King's wife, who is called Donna Giovanna in memory of the Mother of our father, so that he may bear in mind to pray to our Lord that He will preserve in this king the faith he has professed to the greater honour and glory of our Divine Master, and the salvation of so many souls.

Sent to the city of Goa by the order of the same King of Monomotapa, &c.

Copy of a Letter from the Rev. Fr. Thomas de Barros to the Provincial at Portugal.

GOA, *February* 27, 1630.

The Emperor Monomotapa has been made a Christian and tributary to the King of Portugal. This great service to God and religion has been the work of Fr. Louis of the Holy Ghost, who in war and peace has been the chief figure and agent; it is he who has baptised the King, &c.

Copy of a Letter from the Rev. Fr. Geronimo of the Passion, Deputy from the Holy Office to the Provincial of Portugal.

GOA, *February* 20, 1630.

In this vessel there is going by order of the Vice-

Regent of this state, one of our Catechumens. He is sent that he may be placed in a monastery of St. Dominic, either that of your Reverence, or in that of the Rev. Prior, in order that, according to the wish of his Majesty, he may be baptised with all pomp and state, either by the hand of your Reverence, or whose ever the King may command, because he is a prince and hereditary heir of him who was emperor of the great *Mancura* empire of Monomotapa. And he is nephew of him who is vassal of His Majesty, and who has been made Emperor, and whom we have baptised. Therefore it will be well that your Reverence shall cause our Catechumen to be placed by order of the King in some Dominican Convent, and be baptised with all pomp and ceremony. And he should be given such state and accommodation as is befitting a prince of so great an empire as *Mancura*, so that the kingdom and Court of Spain, and that of Rome, may know that the sons of St. Dominic have taken in hand, and baptised emperors, and sons and nephews of emperors.

Ibid. p. 38.   *Advices from Goa of* 1630.   *Monomotapa.*

The Emperor of Monomotapa having robbed the Portuguese residing in Sena and Tete, and killed the Ambassador whom the Captain at Mozambique had sent to him, we took the field with two hundred and fifty Portuguese and thirty thousand Kafirs, their vassals, at two different times—the first in December, 1628, and the second in May, 1629. Their two great armies were destroyed, and on the second day the greater part of the grandees of the empire were killed, and the remainder made Manura their emperor in place of the former one, who, according to the laws of the country, for certain excesses he had committed in the flight, could no longer reign. Manura at this time became a Christian, and was put in possession by the Portuguese, in the name of and as the vassal of their king, and received and guaranteed all the conditions which the Portuguese considered conformable to the honour of the Gospel, and of the Crown of Portugal.

<small>Lettere Volgari, 1630, vol. x., p. 146.</small> The Holy Congregation of the Propaganda writes to Monsig. Colletore of Portugal :—

ROME, *December* 31, 1630.

Your letter of the 12th of October last with advices from India sent to this Holy Congregation has been passed on to Cardinal Barberino, and to Cardinal Trevultio. Their Eminences have heard with much pleasure and satisfaction of the great work done by those Religious of Portugal in these immense and distant parts of the world for the propagation of our Holy Faith. After having highly commended their labours and diligence in this holy and divine work, they have commissioned me to write when opportunity occurs and notify to their superiors in religion, the pleasure they have in hearing of the progress of their fathers, and to ask them at the same time, to give them news from time to time, so that they may be able to communicate it to the same Holy Congregation. That it may not be without merit and glory to their religion, their acts should be given to this Holy Congregation, in which the History of the Church is written, and in which will be noted the most worthy actions of the Portuguese Fathers.

I write and inclose with this a duplicate to Fr. Louis of the Holy Ghost, and from this, which is sent open, your Reverence will see what has been done to obtain for him some advance in his Order. We send this in order that you may send it to him to encourage and animate him in the work of the conversion of Monomotapa.

Ibid. p. 147. The Sacred Congregation of Propaganda writes to Fr. Louis of the Holy Ghost Dominican:—

ROME, *December* 31, 1630.

It having been reported to this Sacred Congregation of the Propagation of the Faith that your Reverence has by the help of God done a great work in the conversion of the Emperor of Monomotapa, their Eminences the Monsignori have heard of this with great pleasure, after having highly commended your honourable labours, they have desired me in their names to thank you (which I do most heartily), and at the same time to pray you to persevere in the important work of the conversion of this Empire which has been so well begun, and to let them know, as often as possible, the progress that is made. And as your Reverence's merits are shown in these acts, they have written to the General of your Order, asking him to encourage and animate you in these great labours in the service of God, by conferring on you such advance as is usual in the Order. And this will no doubt be done in conformity with the request of these Cardinals. In whose name have the kindness to salute and revere the Emperor, and offer him any service in their power to do for him here. In conclusion, I beg to wish your Reverence every blessing, &c.

Original letters, 1631, vol. 99, p. 12. The Colletore of Portugal, Monsig. Lorenzo, Bishop of Gerace, Lisbon, June 28, 1631:—

I send with this, to your Eminence, the accounts which

we have had from a Dominican Father of the state of Christianity in the kingdom of Monomotapa and the rest of Africa on the other side of the Cape of Good Hope, where one may say there is an immense harvest and few workers, which your Eminence will gather from the enclosed.

The kingdom of Monomotapa is very large and full of people, nearly all Pagans, and without knowledge of religion. It is rich in gold mines, ebony, and ivory. And in the opinion of many it is the ancient Ophir, where Solomon sent his ships, which sailed through the Red Sea to the Coast of Africa. A very easy navigation and full of ports.

Monomotapa.

The extent of the kingdom is not known, but it is believed to be bounded on one side by the kingdom of Angola, and on the other by that of Prester John.

In this kingdom the Portuguese hold possession of many places near the sea and an immense number in the interior; of these we shall tell briefly all that is known at present.

I shall commence with the city of Sofala, which, beyond the Cape of Good Hope is the first we find inhabited by Christians. It is a fortress of the King of Portugal, governed by a Portuguese Hidalgo, subject to the Governor of Mozambique. There are about a hundred Christian families, between Portuguese, Mulatto, and Negroes, as well as others, Pagans.

Sofala.

There is only one Dominican church here with one or two priests, no other friars.

This is a place without power. None are made Christians who are not born so. We have baptised many of the natives, but they do not live as Christians, because there is no one to take care of them.

Chilimani — Has a modern fortress called Chimbo, which is the seat of a Portuguese Presidency. There is a small wooden church with one father of the Society. The people are Mahometans and Pagans.

Luabo — Is an island where there is another fortress and several native and Portuguese Christians. The island is three leagues in circumference, the inhabitants are also black. There is one Church of St. Dominic, with one father. From Quilimani as far as the river there are many Christians, of whom no one takes charge. But there are many who come from Sena to explore, but they seek only gold.

Sena — Is a fortress of the King, seven days' journey towards the interior. It has more than two hundred Christian houses. There is a parochial church, where they have ten priests. The Church of St. Dominic with three or four friars. Also the Church of St. Anthony in charge of a priest.

Beyond Sena is a Christian settlement called Laruntuca, **Laruntuca.** where there is a church named "Our Lady of Remedy," belonging to the Dominicans. It has one priest, under whom there are other villages, in each of which there are Christians.

Tete — Is a fortress above Sena towards the river, about a hundred leagues from the sea. There are about one hundred Christian families, Portuguese and natives. The principal church is Dominican, with two fathers, and there is another Church of Fathers of the Society, which has also two fathers. Under these are many country places where there are Christians subject to the aforesaid. All these places are under the King.

Luanze, One hundred and sixty leagues from the sea. There are ten or twelve Christian families here, the rest are Pagans. *And here begins the land of Gold.* It has a Dominican church with one father.

Bambarare, Two hundred and twenty leagues from the sea. The people have made a mart here, and many come here to buy gold. It has a Dominican church with one friar.

Mazapa, Another town similar to the above with a similar church.

Zimbaoe Is the royal city of Monomotapa, very near the above named Mazapa. It is said to be a very great city. There is no church here, but there are many Christians, who are refugees. The monks cannot come here as they are not able to pay the King the submission and adoration which he exacts from all.

Turning towards the sea we find a place called Manica, which belongs to the King of Ochetene, who is great and powerful. Here are many Portuguese and native Christians. It has a Dominican church with two priests. There are several villages round about in which there are Christians.

Matura. About forty or fifty Christians, and a Dominican church and priest.

Maungo. A village under the above-named priest.

Abunda. Containing ten or twelve Portuguese and some native Christians. There is a church, but no priest. One should be provided. There are many little villages and places subject to the King of Ochetene where there are Christians with no pastor. They are about seven days' journey from the sea. In each of these places there are chiefs of the people,

APPENDIX B. 237

Christian deputies from the Ministers of the Portuguese king. From here we go by coast to Mozambique, which is the principal station of the Portuguese in these parts, with a large port used by the ships from India.

Mozambique, A fortress in which is stationed a Portuguese Hidalgo as General, who is also Governor of Sofala, and to the river of Cuama. It has a Collegiate church with eight or nine clerics. A Dominican Monastery with seven friars. Another of the fathers of the Society with ten or twelve religious. Also a hermitage of St. Anthony outside the city. The Portuguese population numbers about 150, besides the residents of the fortress, who are more than 100 men. There are also many native Christians living here, and on the other side of the mouth of the river.

Chirimba, An island on the north of Mozambique about two leagues in circumference. It has a population of thirty or forty Portuguese besides the natives of the country, all Christians. There is one Dominican church with two friars.

Ibo, Another island with a like church and one friar. Round about this island are others, but without churches, and under the rule of the friars at Chirimba. There are many other residences of the Dominican fathers, and of the Society from the province of Mozambique, similar to those spoken of above.

Below Mozambique, on the sea coast, is another city called Mombasa, where there is a fortress **Mombasa.** likewise belonging to the King of Portugal, and inhabited by Portuguese; and below Mombasa, towards the Red Sea, is the City of Quiloa.

Quiloa. Like the others, a fortress of the same king. And in the environs and precincts of these cities are spread many Christians as in other parts already named. The temporal dominion belongs to various native rulers. The Spiritual dominion of this as well as the other places spoken of all belongs to the Archbishop of Goa, who is distant more than a thousand leagues from the Cape of Good Hope. This Prelate is Ordinary of all the Christians there.

The Sacred Congregation of Propaganda writes to the Colletore of Portugal, February 14, 1631 :—

Letters, 1631 and 1632, vol. ii. p. 6.

With this we send to your Lordship the letters patent from the General of the Dominicans for presentation to Fr. Louis of the Holy Ghost, of which he will be able to make use of extracts, so that if the originals do not arrive he may at least have these within reach. And your Lordship will desire this father to send to you a full account of the Kingdom of Monomotapa, of the adjacent country, of the fruit which has resulted from his labours, of what can be done there, and of the spiritual needs which follow from the conversion of this kingdom. When your lordship has received this send it to this Sacred Congregation.

The Sacred Congregation of Propaganda writes to the Colletore of Portugal, November 20, 1631 :—

Ibid. p. 122.

The letters of your Lordship concerning the kingdom of Monomotapa and the other residences of Religious on the coast of Africa beyond the Cape of Good Hope have been referred to the Sacred Congregation. Their Eminences having heard of the paucity of Religious in those parts, desire that your Lordship shall communicate with those religious orders, who have knowledge and experience of these places upon the best means of providing ecclesiastical labourers, and let this Sacred Congregation know what they advise.

<small>Original letters, 1632, vol. 74, p. 199.</small> Monsig. Lorenzo, Bishop of Gerace, writes to the Propaganda:—

LISBON, *November* 1, 1631.

I have urged the Archbishop of Goa, who is at the Court of Madrid, to do all he can to procure Missionaries, and he writes to me by last post that His Majesty has made a concession of eighteen for the parts of Monomotapa, when so many are found willing to go, they will be of great assistance in those parts.

<small>Ibid. p. 192.</small> The above named writes:—

LISBON, *May* 1, 1632.

I cannot report to your Eminence that arrangements have been made for the four Franciscan Capuchins to go as Missionaries to Monomotapa because the Procurator is at present on visitation, and I am advised to wait for him to select them. It is best that he should choose them, and advise the time of their departure to your Eminence. So that the Mission cannot be ready until next year, it being too late for this.

I have endeavoured to procure a detailed map of the kingdom of Monomotapa, but have not yet found one. I have got in this place a book by a Dominican from which can be drawn much information about this and other kingdoms of Africa and Asia, in the matter of the Faith and its propagation. I have thought of sending it to your Eminence, which I do.

APPENDIX B.

Letters, &c., vol. xii. p. 5, 1632. The Propaganda writes to the Colletore of Portugal, January 31, 1632:—

The news that two Missionaries are designated to go to the Mine and Monomotapa is very pleasing to this Sacred Congregation. They desire that when it is settled your Lordship will send them the names, surnames, and countries of the religious who are going to these parts, and in particular the names of the Prefects of these Missionaries, who should in every way be appointed by their superiors, because Missionaries under superiors receive most fruit, and your Lordship can better keep up correspondence so as to be advised of the progress of their Missions, and report to this Sacred Congregation.

APPENDIX C.

Biblioth. Vatican. Cod. Othob. lat. 2416, f. 899.

Written in the year 1699 *or* 1700.

I.

THE MONOMOTAPA OR KAFIR MISSION.

More than forty years ago this mission was begun by P. Gonsalvo Silveira, who carried it to such success that he baptised the King of Monomotapa, his (the King's) mother and three hundred of the *élite*. Unfortunately his mission ended with his life, which he lost through the snares (intrigues) of Aligamus a Mahometan prelate. On the fourth of the nones of February last year, seven of the Society (of Jesus) were sent thither with the fleet of Stephen Ataydius, which followed a very difficult route, for when it reached the equinox a most frightful tempest occurred, so that the ship of Ataydius, which was first at scarcely two months' distance from Mozambique, was never again in sight of any of the others. This ship which was saved held three (members) of the

Society. One of these fathers used exhortation with the sailors, and induced them all to go to confession; which they did, whereat also the tempest was calmed. Another of the ships when passing by the reefs of India (?) was stranded by a tide (the force of the sea = *refluente maris æstu*). For an entire day she remained there exposed to great danger, but by the Divine mercy she was brought to the mouth of the river Comorus, and when all had been landed in safety there split in two parts. But the evil plight of the passengers and sailors was only increased (or not altogether lessened) thereby, for they were confronted with the dangers of a savage country without any certain means of escape. Even as they advanced in boats the natives, *i.e.*, the Kafirs and the Moorish (black) princelets laid snares for them. They escaped however from these and arrived at Mozambique. They speedily made an agreement with some of the Moorish (black) princes (sovereigns) on the sea coast that a free passage, entertainment, and free reception should henceforward be given to the Portuguese and to the fathers of the Society of Jesus visiting those lands. This was the first agreement. The second was that they should not Mahometanise any Kafir. The third that the Moors (blacks) should not allow any Kafirs to be sold as slaves. Forthwith they began to erect fortifications for the defence of the Christians, and near to these churches for the Christianisation of the Kafirs. Three Jesuit centres (*collegia*) were then erected for the conversion of the Kafirs; at Mozambique, Sena, and Mochranga.

II.

THE MARTYRDOM OF FATHER SILVEIRA.

Translation from the folio edition in the Vatican of the History of the Society of Jesus.

While these things were going forward prosperously and well, behold the wicked enemy of human kind, playing upon their envy, actively stirred up certain Mahometans, ready for this crime, to destroy the faith of the King. They assembled, therefore, and deliberated upon their purpose. At this meeting was present Mingames, a prince from Mozambique, a wicked man who held the rank of prelate in the Mahometan superstition. It was readily resolved that the first thing to be undertaken was to attempt the death of Gonzalez in every possible way and that everything else depended upon that. Then they gave notice of this by letters, and employed as messengers to carry the news the other members of the same sect who dwelt at Sena in the kingdom of Sofala and those who dwelt in the places and islands bordering upon the great river Cuama. Further, they decided to put together a respectable sum of money wherewith to set the King's mind against Gonzalez in case craft, lying, and false accusations should fail of their purpose. Lastly, they chose four members of their religion who possessed more favour with the King, and who exceeded the others both in guile and influence. Of these Mingames himself was the first. Then all these accomplished knaves and poisoners hurried to the King feigning the sincerest devotion towards his person, his house, and his entire kingdom, and setting the most wicked snares for the ignorance of Gonzalez. It is incredible to what lengths they went in the assertion of their power over him by poisons and incantations. They told the King that he had come into those parts as a spy and not as a friend; that he desired to effect in the kingdom of Monomotapa and in all India and the larger part of Africa what the Langaru (as they called the Portuguese) had wished to do, but that they had invaded the dominions of others under the pretext of friendliness, and that they had subjugated them to their yoke. And if the King wished to see this with his own eyes, and, as it were, to touch it with his own hands, they were able to put him in possession of the proofs. With every contrivance of superstition the King was brought to believe that magic significations evidently revealed that Cacizuis of the Nazarenes (the Saracens call the Christians Nazarenes) had been sent by the Viceroy of India and the Prefect of Sofala to spy in the country of Monomotapa, and that unless he was quickly overcome, the Portuguese army would come to do harm to the King and his kingdom. "Oh, misguided King," they said, "do you hesitate to believe that what we predict is sure to come about if you hasten not to destroy the author of the evil? Do not forget upon what agreement and false understanding these people were allowed to enter into the kingdom of Mozambique, and to violently occupy the kingdom of Sofala which was at first tributary to you. Do you not know that these Langaru have by craft contrived to possess themselves of the sea coast of India? He would be blind indeed who did not perceive that the chief part of this conspiracy is due to Scinpurus, the tyrant of Sofala, who having sacrilegiously, not so long ago, denied you the obedience and submission due, has gone over to the Langaru. Do you not feel that the mind of the people is being led to treason by this false liberality? What is the scope of that simulated piety with which this most astute impostor distributed to the populace, as by an act of mercy, the oxen which you had presented to him? Recognise all this guile; plots are being hatched against you with your very gifts." Thus induced, the sovereign gave orders for the immediate death of Gonzalez. This holy man was divinely illuminated as to his impending fate, as he revealed in a beautiful declaration to Antonius Caiandus, asserting his innocence and fearlessness before death. Thereupon this person (Antonius Caiandus) went to the King and used most powerful exhortation to avert death from Gonzalez, pointing out to the sovereign that he had been deceived by his counsellors, that the death of Gonzalez would greatly offend the King of Portugal and the Viceroy of India, and that Gonzalez was moreover innocent. But it was all to no avail. The King was unmoved. The only reply which he made was that he would re-examine the question in the presence of the Engaga (that was the name of the Mahometans). Realising the issue of such a conference Antonius Caiandus returned to Gonzalez and admonished him that his death was inevitable. Gonzalez's flight was then resolved upon, and its method determined; the whole plan being kept in absolute secrecy. Then Antonius Caiandus returned to the King and pleaded a second time. Unfortunately the answers of the King and of his mother were deceptive. Nevertheless when he returned to Gonzalez, and spoke hopefully of the reply which had been given him at Court, Gonzalez remained undeceived, unmoved in his consciousness that death was imminent. Therefore he called to him two or three Portuguese from a neighbouring village, and expressed his wish to hear their confession and to give them Holy Communion as later he would be unable to do so. (The Mass is then described with some detail.) At it he baptised about fifty Kafirs (*Cafres*) whom he had previously instructed, and gave them clothing and rosaries. Antonius Caiandus returned towards night-time. "Why are you so anxious in my regard?" said Gonzalez, I am readier to die than my enemies are desirous of killing me. I willingly forgive the King in the first place, and the mother of the King; he is a youth and she is a woman, and both might easily have been deceived by the Saracens." Then he prayed to God that no vengeance should be taken for his death, but that it should be an atonement for the crime which caused it. When alone, after Antonius Caiandus had gone home, he knelt before the image of the Crucified, and sighing begged Christ from the depths of his heart that all the rage of the barbarians might be allowed to be poured out against him. Rising from prayer, refreshed in soul, he regretted that his hour had not come. He therefore prayed again on his knees before the Crucified, entreating that the cruelty of the barbarians should not be restrained if they should torture his body. Finally, feeling that his time was at hand, he rose and left the place where he had stayed (literally, lodging-house) in order that, like Christ, he should go forth and meet them coming to him. Forthwith he began to walk in the area (open place), and with his eyes fixed always on heaven, sometimes with his hands lifted up and at other times crossed upon his breast, holding most sweet converse with God, sighing and moaning. And when the night had advanced, and his enemies had not yet come (for they had been in a hiding-place near by, and had not dared to disturb him while he walked and kept watch) tired out, he returned to his room, and on his bed of reeds placed the image of Christ which he surrounded with lighted candles. Here amidst his prayers and aspirations he lay down and slept through sheer fatigue. The foe, who had come there in the meantime, perceived him, rushed suddenly upon him and took away his life. There were about eight of them in all. Of these the chief for wealth and other advantages was Macrumes, a Pagan by race and religion, but very well known to Gonzalez, and his familiar at table and in conversation. He was the Judas and the leader of the others. Rushing at Gonzalez first of all the others, he roughly seized his chest. Then, quickly the other four seized his hands and feet and held him. The others threw a rope around his neck, and pulling it violently on either side, put an end to his life. Thus died Gonzalez in the manner which he had often predicted in Portugal, and in the year of grace 1561 on the day after the Ides of March, on the fourth Sunday in Lent. This Sunday is called the Sunday of Susanna in Portugal, because the history of Susanna is sung on the previous Saturday. It is on this account that some one has written that Gonzalez died on the feast of St. Susanna, Virgin and Martyr. The body of the holy man was dragged to the neighbouring river Mosengessis, or, as I find in other authorities, Motes (*Motetem* in the Latin accusative) after the fashion of the natives. Into this river the murderers hurled it. Why? Not because the Mahometans imagined that the exposure of the corpse would cause corruption, but that fulfilment should be given to a prophecy, for Gonzalez had predicted that for Christ's name he should be choked by his enemies, and that his body should be hurled into a river whence it would never reappear. It is said that many lizards (I put this literal form of *lacertos*) of monstrous size and voracity live in that river. They are crocodiles. (The author here narrates their taste for human flesh.) But before the murderers had cast it in, actuated by sordid greed, they stripped it; which doing they found a shirt of mail attached to the skin. In their surprise at so novel a thing they conceived that whoever should use such a shirt of mail must be a noted (*insignis*) poisoner. Nor were these affronts all. The wretched men wreaked their rage on the body of the martyr, nay, on the very image of Christ, taking which, after countless insults, they cut it into pieces and trampled it under foot.

The King learned that fifty men had been baptised by Gonzalez just before his death. He was very wrathful and ordered them to be killed at once. When this order had gone forth, the Lucazes, who are the leading people in the kingdom, went to him and said that if the baptism of these men was to be the cause of their death, that he (the King) and they (the Lucazes) also merited this penalty. The King thereupon relinquished his design. The Mahometans made great rejoicings over the death of Gonzalez, and the defection of the sovereign from the Christian faith, and transmitted the news to all their fellow religionists throughout the entire Kafir district *(in tota Cafraria)*. God avenged the death of His servant, and in this respect were fulfilled predictions uttered by the holy man before his death. Public calamities ensued. A vast invasion of locusts appeared and destroyed every fruit of the earth. Innumerable murders followed and finally the King, comparable to Nero for his cruel disposition, ordered his mother's life to be taken, because she had not repelled the Mahometans who had conspired for his death. For the same reason four of the King's counsellors were condemned to death; two of them were killed at once; two sought safety in flight.

III.

"PORTENTS." EXTRAORDINARY MANNER IN WHICH THE BODY OF FATHER SILVEIRA WAS GUARDED BY BIRDS AND BEASTS.

Biblioteca Apostolica Vaticana.

The writer refers to P. (Father) Alphonsus Leo de Barbudas as his authority, and says that his sworn testimony is of quite infinite value to him. Also to the "Historia Societatis Jesu," &c. (as mentioned on last page of the original manuscript). It seems that Father Alphonsus was obliged to go into the Kingdom of Monomotapa on public business, and that while navigating the Mozambique he was brought by a mere casual storm at sea to that part of the coast of Kafirland where dwell the Opandæ and Nobunquæ,* above the Cape of Good Hope. Thence flows the river which, arising in the Mountains of the Moon, traverse the kingdom of Monomotapa and, for it is the chief river of Kafirland, pours out into the Zambesi. Hither was Alphonsus brought. Entering the Zambesi by the river towards sundown he came to a place where the river is divided and obliged to flow over two separate beds by reason of certain obstacles. Here he made a halt and, having fastened his ship to the bank of the river nearest to him, resolved to await the dawn of

* *Leucis.*

day lest he should founder on the rocks which are so numerous in the river, and which have so often proved fatal by night-time. There was a dense wood, enriched with varied and highly-developed trees in the strip of land which created a division in the river. On the edge of the wooded bank lay an iron-coloured beam (trunk) which formed a receptacle of birds of unknown class, but of exquisite beauty. Their bodies were of resplendent and snowy whiteness, except only the joining of the wings which contrasted in its glinting blackness with their curious red and purple feet. The author notes the curious detail that they wore elevated combs which consisted of five points almost arranged in cross-wise shape (*i.e.*, as a cross). Our father was very much impressed, especially as he learned from the natives that there were others much more beautiful, which might be seen and heard in the early morning. These he heard early next morning. But the fishers who were there added to his wonder by saying that those birds observed a curious law by which a certain part of their number was always stationed on the same trunk, or that when that watch went away it was replaced by another. He gave himself an opportunity of experimenting as to the truth of their assertion and discovered it to be perfectly true. There were three Kafir youths with Father Alphonsus, and these, impelled by curiosity, wished to go prying into the wood, but the fishermen dissuaded them saying that if they approached any nearer some disaster would certainly befall them. The reason for this was, according to the fishermen, that the entrances of the wood were *carefully* guarded by tigers and other savage beasts so that they allowed nobody to put his foot inside the wood. Father Alphonsus asked the cause of this strange fact. They in answer produced this history which they said had circulation among their people. Once upon a time there had come the corpse of a white man wearing a dark tunic (dress), and fastened to that trunk. When it was being borne along by the force of the water it had stuck against the projecting bank. Straightway tigers and crowds of other beasts had hurried from the interior of the wood, had broken the trunk, and leaving the *retinacula* (anything which binds) on the bank had carried the body inland. From that day the birds began to rest on that trunk, the beasts had begun to regularly promenade *(obambulare)* the shore lest any part of the sacred place should suffer violation. They alleged that there still existed eye-witnesses of the fact, for it had occurred about sixty years before. Even then (to-day) the common opinion was that the man whose corpse that was, was a most excellent person, perhaps even one of the minor gods, since even the brutes honoured his corpse. A very old man added to this account that one of the neighbouring rulers had been anxious to learn the cause of this curious fact. He caused the beasts to be attracted by a loud and discordant noise to a particular part of the wood, and two agile youths were made to climb a very high tree. Then they saw a corpse lying on a plain dressed as a Portuguese priest and resembling the same in the face. Several tigers and other fierce beasts kept watch by turn around the body. The youths remained all day in the tree and satisfied their curiosity, and were then able to get down by the aid of the same ruse which had enabled them to come there. Hearing this Father Alphonsus made up his mind that this was the body of Father Gonsalvo Silveira whom the Monomotapans had killed sixty years previously through hatred of the

Christian name. The circumstances of place, time, dress, and all the evidences (*documenta*) showed this. Moreover, while Gonsalvo lived, he had predicted more than once, it is said, that if any one was killed in the royal city of Monomotapa, the Christians should not obtain possession of his body. This, too, strengthened the conclusion of Father Alphonsus. Returning, therefore, to Lisbon he explained all this to the King, and said he was ready to recover the body at whatever peril to himself, but this was never done. "But leaving Africa at last, let us enter Asia."

APPENDIX D.

CROSSES ERECTED BY PORTUGUESE MARINERS ON THE AFRICAN COAST.

These are so interesting to antiquarians that we publish specimen copies of these monuments. They were erected at various points on the coast of the Cape Colony, as well as to the eastward and westward.

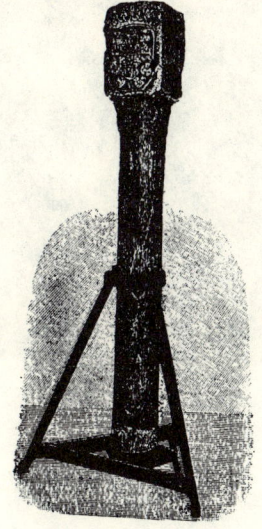

FIG. 1. CROSS ERECTED BY DIAGO CAM.

254   APPENDIX D.

Figures 2, 3, 4, and 5 show the four faces of Fig. 1.

Fig. 2.

APPENDIX D. 255

Fig. 3.

The inscription is—

    Era da c'a
    çã do mund(o)
    d(e) seis mil
    bj̄ lxxxj ano
    do naciment° d(e)
    (N)oso Sor Jhū

In modern Portuguese—

    Era da crea-
    coa do mundo
    de seis mil
    681 anno
    do nascimento de
    Nosso Senhor Jesus Christo

256   APPENDIX D.

Fig. 4.

In modern Portuguese—

de mil quatro centos
82 annos, o
mui atto mui
excellente e pode
roso principe
el Rei D. João

APPENDIX D. 257

Fig. 5.

In modern Portuguese—

Sequndo, de Por
tugal mandou
descobrir esta
terra e pôr
estes padroes,
por Diogo Cão, escudeiro
de sua cara

FIG. 6. PORTUGUESE CROSS ERECTED ON WEST COAST.
(*From a photograph sent to Lisbon by the Governor of Angola.*)

APPENDIX D. 259

Fig. 7. PORTUGUESE CROSS ERECTED ON WEST COAST.
(*From a photograph sent to Lisbon by the Governor of Angola.*)

The inscription on it is—

O navegador portuguez, Diogo Cam, erigiu n'este sitio, no anno de 1486, reinando D. João Q.º de Portugal o padrão denominado de Santo Agostinho em memoria do descobremento e Senhoria d'esta costa. Os restos do primitivo padrão foram recolhidas no Museu Colonial de Lisboa no anno de 1891 em que se collocou este padrão.

DATE DUE

WITHDRAWN
from
Funderburg Library

FUNDERBURG LIBRARY

MANCHESTER COLLEGE

916.89
W6 88m